Political Myth

Key Concepts in Political Science

GENERAL EDITOR: Leonard Schapiro

EXECUTIVE EDITOR: Peter Calvert

Other titles in the same series include:

ALREADY PUBLISHED

Martin Albrow	**Bureaucracy**
Anthony H. Birch	**Representation**
Brian Chapman	**Police State**
Peter Calvert	**Revolution**
Ioan Davies	**Social Mobility and Political Change**
Joseph Frankel	**National Interest**
Carl J. Friedrich	**Tradition and Authority**
P. H. Partridge	**Consent and Consensus**
John Planenatz	**Ideology**
John C. Rees	**Equality**
Leonard Schapiro	**Totalitarianism**
Paul Wilkinson	**Social Movement**

IN PREPARATION

Shlomo Avineri	**Utopianism**
Karl Deutsch	**Legitimacy**
S. E. Finer	**Dictatorship**
Geoffrey Goodwin	**International Society**
Julius Gould	**Violence**
J. F. Lively	**Democracy**
Otto Pick and Julian Critchley	**Collective Security**

Political Myth

Henry Tudor

Praeger Publishers
New York · Washington · London

Published in the United States of America in 1972
Praeger Publishers, Inc.
111 Fourth Avenue, New York, N.Y. 10003, U.S.A.
5 Cromwell Place, London, SW7, England

© 1972 by The Pall Mall Press
Library of Congress Catalog Card Number: 77–100927

Printed in Great Britain

Contents

Chapter Five

'Key Concepts'
an Introductory Note

Political concepts are part of our daily speech—we abuse 'bureaucracy' and praise 'democracy', welcome or recoil from 'revolution'. Emotive words such as 'equality', 'dictatorship', 'élite' or even 'power' can often, by the very passions which they raise, obscure a proper understanding of the sense in which they are, or should be, or should not be, or have been used. Confucius regarded the 'rectification of names' as the first task of government. 'If names are not correct, language will not be in accordance with the truth of things', and this in time would lead to the end of justice, to anarchy and to war. One could with some truth point out that the attempts hitherto by governments to enforce their own quaint meanings on words have not been conspicuous for their success in the advancement of justice. 'Rectification of names' there must certainly be: but most of us would prefer such rectification to take place in the free debate of the university, in the competitive arena of the pages of the book or journal.

Analysis of commonly used political terms, their reassessment or their 'rectification', is, of course, normal activity in the political science departments of our universities. The idea of this series was indeed born in the course of discussion between a few university teachers of political science, of whom Professor S. E. Finer of Manchester University was one. It occurred to us that a series of short books, discussing the 'Key Concepts' in political science would serve two purposes. In universities these books could provide the kind of brief political texts which might be of assistance to students in gaining a fuller understanding of the terms which they were constantly using. But we also hoped that outside the universities there exists a reading public which has the time, the curiosity and the inclination to pause to reflect on some of those words and ideas which are so often taken for granted. Perhaps even 'that insidious and crafty animal', as Adam Smith described the politican and statesman, will occasionally derive some pleasure or even profit from that more leisurely analysis which academic study can afford, and which a busy life in the practice of politics often denies.

It has been very far from the minds of those who have been concerned in planning and bringing into being the 'Key Concepts' series to try and impose (as if that were possible!) any uniform pattern on the authors who have contributed, or will contribute, to it. I, for one, hope that each author will, in his own individual manner, seek and find the best way of helping us to a fuller understanding of the concept which he has chosen to analyse. But whatever form the individual exposition may take, there are, I believe, three aspects of illumination which we can confidently expect from each volume in this series. First, we can look for some examination of the history of the concept, and of its evolution against a changing social and political background. I believe, as many do who are concerned with the study of political science, that it is primarily in history that the explanation must be sought for many of the perplexing problems of political analysis and judgement which beset us today. Second, there is the semantic aspect. To look in depth at a 'key concept' necessarily entails a study of the name which attached itself to it; of the different ways in which, and the different purposes for which, the name was used; of the way in which in the course of history the same name was applied to several concepts, or several names were applied to one and the same concept; and, indeed, of the changes which the same concept, or what appears to be the same concept, has undergone in the course of time. This analysis will usually require a searching examination of the relevant literature in order to assess the present stage of scholarship in each particular field. And thirdly, I hope that the reader of each volume in this series will be able to decide for himself what the proper and valid use should be of a familiar term in politics, and will gain, as it were, from each volume a sharper and better-tempered tool for political analysis.

There are many today who would disagree with Bismarck's view that politics can never be an exact science. I express no opinion on this much debated question. But all of us who are students of politics—and our numbers both inside and outside the universities continue to grow —will be the better for knowing what precisely we mean when we use a common political term.

London School of Economics   Leonard Schapiro
and Political Science   General Editor

Preface

This is an introductory book. Its purpose is simply to draw attention to a common but neglected type of political argument, and it is aimed at the educated layman and, more particularly, at the university undergraduate. I am conscious of the fact that it reads a bit like a guided tour, but, given the purpose of this series and the nature of my topic, I could not see how else to approach the task.

In the first two chapters I expound and criticize various theories that have been put forward to explain the occurrence and character of mythical thought. The need to be brief has sometimes led me to state dogmatically points which really require elaborate qualification, and I have dismissed somewhat brusquely the doctrines of many deservedly famous men. However, although I have simplified, I have not, I think, misrepresented the positions I criticize. Great men are, in any case, fair game, and it is unlikely that their reputations will be damaged by any injustice I might unwittingly have done them.

I have devoted the whole of chapter three to a study of the Roman Foundation Myth partly because it has exercised so enduring an influence on Western political thought and partly because it is the 'purest' example of a political myth I could find. Chapter four deals with a number of more recent political myths which, in contrast to foundation myths, I have described as eschatological or revolutionary myths. It goes without saying that each one of them could (and indeed should) have been subjected to at least as detailed a treatment as the Roman Foundation Myth; but space did not permit. The fifth and final chapter raises, though it does not resolve, several questions concerning the relationship of political myth to practical experience.

I have, wherever possible, used recent and easily available editions. Except where indicated, translations from works in foreign languages are my own. All quotations from classical authors are taken from the Loeb Classical Library editions.

My intellectual debts are many, and I will not attempt to acknowledge them. I must, however, thank Professor Schapiro for his helpful editorial suggestions, Mr Bernard Mullins of the Pall Mall Press for his patient encouragement, and Mrs E. Manning and Mrs C. Bates for performing so cheerfully the hideously boring task of typing up my manuscript.

Chapter One

The study of political myths

The question as to what constitutes a political myth is surrounded by too much confusion to be capable of a short answer. However, we can make a start by disposing of a widely held but misleading preconception. In common usage, the term 'myth' stands for any belief that has no foundation in fact. A myth, we are told, is a fiction or illusion, the product of fantasy and wishful thinking rather than the result of any serious attempt to tackle the world in which we live; and political myths are simply fictions or illusions about political matters. There is nothing wrong with using the term in this popular sense—provided that it is used as a term of abuse and with no pretensions to academic rigour. The student of politics is, of course, entitled to regard a given set of beliefs as being false; but it is not his business to denounce such beliefs. His business is to determine what kind of belief they are, to examine their logical structure and to explain why the men who hold them take them to be true. And, in this enterprise, it is as vague as it is tendentious to use the term 'myth' as a synonym for 'illusion'. There are as many different kinds of illusion as there are kinds of belief. Indeed, some would argue that, since any practical understanding entails an abstraction from and therefore a distortion of reality, *all* practical beliefs are fundamentally illusory. Whether or not we wish to go this far, it is clear that, if we are to use the term 'myth' with any precision, we must give it a meaning which enables us to distinguish beliefs which are myths from beliefs which are not.

Unfortunately, this is by no means an easy task. It is true that classicists, folk-lorists and anthropologists take the term to stand for a reasonably well-defined class of traditional tales. But the literature on myths (in this sense) is extraordinarily diverse and difficult to evaluate. Since the time of Plato, the myths of classical antiquity have been the subject of detailed investigation, and, in the nineteenth century, the work of the early ethnographers broadened the field to include the myths of contemporary savages. Since then, specialists in a variety of disciplines have regarded myths as falling within their province. Some have appropriated mythology as a subdivision of comparative linguistics; others have seen myths as a form of religious feeling; Freud and Jung have developed a psychological theory of myth; Cassirer has claimed for myth the status of being a major symbolic form; and social anthropologists, from Malinowski to Lévi-Strauss, have used the study of myths to test and illustrate their various points of view. Much of the work done is of considerable value to the student of politics, but not in any direct or obvious way; for the fact is that, until quite recently, expert mythologists have kept to their traditional hunting grounds and have not concerned themselves with the use of myths in political argument. This neglect can, in part, be put down to the diffidence which any specialized knowledge quite rightly breeds. However, it has had the consequence that most theories of myth are based on material drawn from very ancient or very primitive societies, that is, from societies with no significant political experience.

Political myths are, in the nature of the case, a feature of advanced societies; and the study of such myths has been left to historians who have, more often than not, no more than a nodding acquaintance with the specialized literature on mythology. None the less, a great deal of useful work as been done. Cohn and Hobsbawm (among others) have examined the role of eschatological myths in peasant rebellions; Christopher Hill has written about the seventeenth-century English Myth of the Norman Yoke; and Galinsky's *Aeneas, Sicily and Rome* is the latest in a long series of distinguished works on the Roman Foundation Myth. But historians are reluctant to speculate, and none have, so far, offered a general theory of myth comparable with those developed by specialists in other disciplines.

Political scientists have done remarkably little to fill the gap. Indeed, the most interesting attempt to elaborate a notion of political myth is to be found in Sorel's *Reflections on Violence*. Here Sorel is largely concerned with the fact that men engaged in violent popular upheavals often display a degree of courage and readiness for self-sacrifice which cannot be accounted for in narrowly pragmatic terms. Why, after all, should men risk their lives in a cause from which it is obvious they have little or nothing to gain? For Sorel, the answer is clear. Such men, he argues, are not inspired by pragmatic considerations; they are impelled to act by the *pouvoir moteur* of a great myth, a vision which permits them to 'picture their coming action as a battle in which their cause is certain to triumph'.[1] Marx's expectation of a proletarian revolution and the syndicalist notion of the general strike were, in Sorel's view, myths of this kind; and so were the millennialist doctrines of the early Christian Church.

The hallmark of a myth, as Sorel understands it, is that it provides a vision of the future which makes crude but practical sense of the present. It gives men a fixed point by reference to which they can express their feelings and explain their experience. Typically, each conflict in the present is seen as a prelude to the decisive battle destined to take place in the future. Catholics, Sorel tells us, 'have always pictured the history of the Church as a series of battles between Satan and the hierarchy supported by Christ; every new difficulty which arises is only an episode in a war which must finally end in the victory of Catholicism'.[2] Similarly, for the syndicalist worker, every industrial conflict becomes a 'vanguard fight', a further step along the road to that apocalypse in which the bourgeoisie will meet its doom.[3] The understanding thus achieved is no doubt of a somewhat uncomplicated kind. It throws all oppositions into sharp relief and leaves no room for what Sorel calls 'the reconciliation of contraries in the equivocations of the professors'.[4] But it has the important advantage that it clarifies the experience of men without stultifying their will to act.

One point that Sorel was particularly anxious to stress was that, although many myths contain Utopian elements, myth as such is not to be confused with Utopian thinking. 'A Utopia is,' he remarked, 'an intellectual product; it is the work of theorists who, after observing and discussing the known facts, seek to establish a model to which they can compare existing society.' Utopias are programmes for reform. They can be discussed 'like any other social constitution', and they can be refuted 'by showing that the economic system on which they have been made to rest is incompatible with the necessary conditions of modern production'. Myths are, in all these respects, quite different. They depict the future, not as a possible social order, but as a catastrophic event. They are 'not descriptions of things, but expressions of a determination to act'.[5] Their purpose is to evoke 'all the strongest inclinations of a people, of a party or of a class, inclinations which recur to the mind with the insistence of instincts in all the circumstances of life'; and their effect is to 'give an aspect of complete reality to the hopes of immediate action by which, more easily than by any other method, men can reform their desires, passions, and mental activity'.[6] In short, so far from containing a list of reforms to be accomplished, a myth 'confronts men with a catastrophe'.[7] And the belief that the catastrophe will indeed take place is not founded on any analysis of the present state of affairs; it arises from the ability of the myth to cast light on the practical experience of those to whom it is addressed. It is, at bottom, a matter of faith; and herein lies its strength. Because a myth has nothing specific to propose and gives no reasons for what it asserts, it eludes the critical efforts of 'intellectualist philosophy'. Unlike a programme or a prediction, a myth cannot be refuted.[8]

Sorel's remarks about myth attracted little attention in the academic world. Certainly, they provoked no significant debate; and, although mythology flourished in other fields, it languished in the study of politics to such a degree that, in 1939, Lasswell could write: 'In recent usage the term "myth" is impartially employed to refer to any words in the name of which social groups undertake to advance or defend their position in society.'[9] Not only has this usage proved far too loose to be helpful (despite Lasswell's later attempts to refine it), but it bears little relationship to what historians and anthropologists nowadays understand by 'myths'. Friedrich and Brzezinski have, however, proposed a more promising alternative. 'A myth,' they say, 'is typically a tale concerned with past events, giving them a special meaning and significance for the present and thereby reinforcing the authority of those who are wielding power in a particular community.'[10] Stalin's retrospective reconstruction of the October Revolution is, in this sense, a myth, as is the Nazi appeal to the alleged Aryan origins of the German people.

Friedrich and Brzezinski's analysis may be too restricted in the material it considers; but it does point us in the right direction. To begin with, Sorel's notion of a myth as the vision of a future catastrophe excludes from being myths all doctrines that are not clearly eschatological in character. The Roman Foundation Myth, for example, does not fit Sorel's definition, and neither does the Myth of the Norman Yoke, the Afrikaaner Myth of the Great Trek or the American Myth of the Founding Fathers. In all these myths, there is indeed a critical event by reference to which men can order their present experience, but the events in question are thought of as having taken place in the past. The view suggested by Friedrich and Brzezinski at least allows us to include these doctrines as being genuine myths.

But more important than this is the emphasis they place on two points which most contemporary mythologists would regard as crucial to any adequate notion of myth: they insist that a myth is told, not for the sake of amusement, but in order to promote some practical purpose; and they make it clear that a myth is, by definition, a story, that is, a narrative of events in dramatic form. It will serve us well to bear these points in mind, for much of the discussion that follows will be devoted to investigating their implications. For the moment, however, let me stress that, though a myth is always a story, it is not for this reason a piece of pure fiction. The Norman invasion of England, the American War of

Independence and the Great Trek of the Afrikaaners are all events that actually took place; but this has not prevented them from being made the subjects of political myths. A myth, I suggest, is an interpretation of what the myth-maker (rightly or wrongly) takes to be hard fact. It is a device men adopt in order to come to grips with reality; and we can tell that a given account is a myth, not by the amount of truth it contains, but by the fact that it is *believed* to be true and, above all, by the dramatic form into which it is cast.

It remains only to add that there is, from a formal point of view, nothing distinctive about a political myth. The kinds of assumption and reasoning found in political myths are the same as those found in any other kind. What marks a myth as being political is its subject matter. Just as nature myths deal with natural phenomena and religious myths deal with gods and their worship, so political myths deal with politics. The study of political myths is, in other words, a branch of general mythology; and if our understanding of political myths is to be soundly based, it must take into account, not only the greatest possible variety of examples, but also what mythologists have said concerning the nature of mythical thought as such.

Allegorical and Euhemerist theories of myth

In classical antiquity, mythological speculation was first provoked by the doubts that had arisen concerning the existence of the gods. Already in the sixth century BC Xenophanes had argued that the gods, as described by Homer and Hesiod, were nothing but fictions which men had fabricated in imitation of their own natures. 'Aethiopians,' he observed, 'have gods with snub noses and black hair, Thracians have gods with grey eyes and red hair.'[11] We cannot say how widely the views of Xenophanes were accepted by his contemporaries; but by the time of Plato, religious scepticism had become the stock-in-trade of philosophers and sophists alike. Democritus, for instance, argued that the men of old conceived of the gods to account for thunder, lightning and other particularly frightening or abnormal natural phenomena. Prodicus maintained that the gods arose through the tendency of primitive men to deify all things they deemed of benefit to human life. The Epicureans held that the ancients derived their notion of the gods from the figures that appeared in their dreams and visions. And, finally, some suggested that, in early times, priests and princes conspired to invent 'both the fancy about the gods and the belief in the mythical events in Hades' in order to keep their turbulent subjects in check.[12]

Although all these views have left their mark on subsequent theorizing about myths, none of them are directly concerned with myths as such. Their aim is to account for the origin of certain obsolete religious beliefs; and their proper place is in the history of religion, not in the study of myths. However, their continued influence on mythological studies is significant, if only because of the confusion it has caused. In particular, it has encouraged the unfortunate view that myths are, by definition, fanciful tales concerning anthropomorphic gods and should be treated as a primitive kind of religious thought. There is much to be said for many of the theories this view has inspired; but, because they all start by defining myth in terms of its content rather than its form, none of them can, in the end, provide a satisfactory account of the way myths work.

Speculation concerning the origin of the gods did, however, produce two theories sufficiently general in scope to merit special attention. Of these, the first to establish itself was the view that myths should be read as allegories concealing an important moral or philosophical point. This view enjoyed a considerable vogue throughout the ancient world, but it was in the schools of the Stoics that it reached its fullest development. The Stoics found that, by identifying the gods with various natural features and forces, they could translate most traditional myths into so many statements of cosmological doctrine.[13] Not only did this endow the findings of natural philosophy with the sanction of hoary antiquity; it also helped vindicate popular religious beliefs by showing that they were, after all, founded on reason. Unfortunately, the Stoics were unable to agree on their interpretations, and all their efforts served only to reveal the arbitrary character of their method. When the time came, Christian apologists, such as Eusebius, had no difficulty discrediting the entire enterprise. The allegorical theory of myth did not, however, perish with the advent of Christianity. On the contrary, it was adopted as a standard technique of biblical exegesis; and thus it survived to flourish again during the Renaissance, finding a distinguished advocate in none other than Francis Bacon. In our own time, a variant of the allegorical view has been revived as part of Bultmann's effort to 'demythologize' Christian doctrine.[14]

The thesis of the allegorist is that, taken as they stand, myths are so absurd that their true meaning must be other than the one which lies on the surface. They must have a hidden meaning which it is the business of the interpreter to elicit. If asked what could have prompted the ancients to hide their meaning in the obscure language of metaphor and parable the allegorist replies that they did so 'either to prevent great truths passing into the hands of persons too ignorant or too impious to use them aright, or to attract by stories those who would not listen to a dry and formal discussion'.[15] Both suggestions are unsatisfactory. They assume the existence of primaeval sages possessed of a systematic body of knowledge, and they assume it (usually) on the basis of no evidence. The method of the allegorist is, in other words, arbitrary. Indeed, although it is easy to show that a given myth can bear the meaning he suggests, it is impossible to show that it can bear no other meaning or that the meaning proposed is the one the original myth-maker intended. The allegorist simply takes it that myths are made by men who think like himself and that, therefore, the meaning he puts upon a myth must be the one intended by the myth's originator.

In classical antiquity, the main alternative to the allegorical view was that of Euhemerus. Like the allegorist, the Euhemerist argues that the literal meaning of a myth cannot be its true meaning; but he differs from the allegorist in his claim that myths must have originated as plain accounts of historical personages and events. If a myth seems incomprehensible to us, this is partly because its contents have suffered distortion in being transmitted and partly because the men of early times had a tendency to deify outstanding individuals and to exaggerate their achievements. Myths, in other words, are not esoteric philosophy but garbled history; and the business of the interpreter is to apply the rules of probability and thus extract the kernel of historical fact which they contain.[16]

The 'historicizing' of myths in the manner of Euhemerus became something of an industry in classical antiquity. The Latin poet, Ennius, translated Euhemerus's *Sacred Histories* and large fragments of this translation were preserved in Lactantius's *Divine Institutes*. During the Renaissance, Euhemerism was temporarily eclipsed by the revival of the allegorical view, but it soon recovered its popularity. In one form or another, it has its advocates even today, and the reasons are not far to seek. Since Schliemann's discovery of Homer's Troy, historians have, with profit, looked again at some of the myths they previously took to be pure fiction, while, in the field of politics, it is abundantly clear that the English Myth of the Norman Yoke, the American Myth of the Founding Fathers and countless other political myths are based on actual historical events.

However, though it is true that many myths do contain a kernel of historical fact, it is equally true that others do not; and herein lies the defect of Euhemerism considered as a general theory of myth. It begs the question, and, for this reason, the results it obtains are often no less arbitrary than those of the allegorist. The same myth may be capable of several different interpretations, and, in the absence of corroborating historical evidence, there is no way of telling which is correct.

This objection was as obvious to the ancients as it is to us. The best of the ancient historians therefore 'Euhemerized' with caution and stressed that any account of the past based on myths alone was bound to be guesswork.[17] Their doubts, however, were not shared by those who had a religious or political axe to grind. Indeed, the very latitude the Euhemerist method allowed meant that myths could be freely interpreted according to the needs of the moment. It was, consequently, in political debate rather than in historical research that Euhemerism found its vocation, and it was here that its true character stood revealed.

I will illustrate the point. During the principate of Augustus, Dionysius of Halicarnassus published his *Roman Antiquities*. The work is an attempt to demonstrate that the early inhabitants of Latium, from whom the Romans traced their descent, were not barbarians but men of true Hellenic stock, and that therefore the Greeks had no good reason to reject the rule of Rome.[18] In the course of his exposition, Dionysius discusses the myth of Hercules and Cacus. This somewhat fanciful tale of how Hercules, by guile and force, recovered the stolen cattle of Geryon contains (according to Dionysius) the memory of an important historical event. Hercules, it appears, was a distinguished Greek general leading a victorious army home from Spain. While they were resting in the plain of Latium and awaiting the arrival of their fleet, Cacus, a local chieftain, raided their camp and made off with some of their cattle. The Greeks mounted a punitive expedition and, in the fight that followed, Cacus himself was killed and his stronghold destroyed. Subsequently, Hercules embarked with his main force, leaving a part of his army to settle among the grateful inhabitants of the district.[19]

Now, it often happens that the practical ideas of previous generations are picked up and modified so that they can be put back into use. Myths are particularly susceptible to this kind of treatment; and the way Dionysius interprets the myth of Hercules and Cacus is a case in point. Dionysius is, of course, aware that the myth was popularly associated with certain very ancient religious rites. This, however, does not interest him. He is not concerned with how the vulgar understand the myth. His business is to discover its 'true' meaning, and this he does by translating it into a plausible historical account. But, in so doing, he has not in any sense explained the myth; nor, indeed, has he proved anything concerning the history of early Latium. He has simply rewritten an old myth with a view to using it in a new controversy. He has put forward, not an interpretation of the myth, but a new mythical argument. And this, I suggest, is what a Euhemerist understanding of myths usually amounts to. It is itself a form of mythical argument, a method whereby old myths are revitalized and made to serve a new purpose.

The Idealist theory of myth

Most Enlightenment mythologists saw no need to go beyond the boundaries set by the Euhemerist point of view. There were, of course, exceptions. Boileau suggested that the origin of myths was to be sought in the ambiguity of language; Fontenelle argued that myths are fundamentally rational attempts by primitive men to explain the world; and, in his *New Science*, Giambattista Vico maintained that the earliest men 'were poets who spoke in poetic characters' and that myths were what survived of their speech.[20] But none of these suggestions received sufficient backing to make it a major school of thought.

In the early nineteenth century, however, the work of the German Idealists introduced a new perspective into the study of myth. Their thesis was (to put it briefly) that what men do is governed by what they think. Consciousness, they maintained, determines existence. As men change their ideas, so they change the way they conduct their lives and order their common affairs. Moreover (it was held) men do not change their ideas haphazardly. Their ideas progress in accordance with an inexorable logic, from the crude to the sublime, from the imperfect to the complete. Human history, in other words, displays a rational development, for it is, at bottom, nothing other than the progressive manifestation or self-realization of Mind or Spirit in the lives of men.

It is sometimes said that German Idealism prepared the ground for the rise of modern totalitarian myths. According to this thesis, the Idealist vision of human affairs as determined by the action of a supra-individual *weltgeist* helped give the state a personality and a destiny which mere individuals might share but which they could never hope to resist. And this, we are told, is the stuff of which the political myths of our time are made. However, before we leap to the conclusion that Hegel invented Hitler, we might recall that, from as far back as our records go, mythical thinking has been a persistent feature of political life. Political myth-makers did not have to await the advent of German Idealism to ply their trade. Besides, there are very few philosophical or scientific doctrines that cannot be refashioned to serve the purposes of mythical argument. The teachings of Hegel may, indeed, lend themselves to being misused in this way, but then so do the doctrines of

Darwin, Marx and Freud. So far as we are concerned, the significance of the Idealist position is that it bred, not a series of totalitarian myths, but a tradition of mythological speculation—a tradition which began with Creuzer and Schelling but found its most lucid expression in the work of J. J. Bachofen.

Bachofen took the view that all history is to be explained in terms of changes in religious beliefs. 'There is,' he said, 'only one mighty lever of all civilization, and that is religion. Every rise and every decline of human existence springs from a movement that originates in this supreme sphere.'[21] With this preconception firmly in mind, he directed his attention to the civilizations of classical antiquity.

Ancient Greek and Roman society was, he argued, patriarchal in character. The father was the founder and head of the family; property was passed from father to son, and so was the family name. Politics and war were male prerogatives, and the official religion was that of the Olympian pantheon, the gods of the sun-lit sky presided over by Zeus the Father. But, in this luminous Apollonian world, Bachofen detected elements which were inconsistent with the general tenor of Hellenic civilization. These, he concluded, must be survivals from an older and radically different culture, a culture the dominating principle of which was mother-right.[22]

In the development of mother-right itself Bachofen distinguished two separate epochs. The earliest, he claimed, was characterized by a state of general sexual promiscuity in which women, children and property were held in common or became the domain of a single individual. Since the woman was the natural parent, the identity of the father being always uncertain, the family was perpetuated in the female line. In religious matters, this stage of culture was associated with the worship of Aphrodite and the spontaneous and untamed generative powers of nature.[23]

The second stage, that of matriarchy proper, came into being with the institution of monogamous marriage, a development which opened the way for the supremacy of women in all spheres of life; for, as Bachofen remarks, 'the matrilinear transmission of property and names is meaningful only where there is marriage'.[24] It was under the auspices of perfected matriarchy that mankind, abandoning its previous nomadic existence, first built settled communities and began to till the soil, while, in religion, the harvest moon and the cult of Demeter replaced the wild and unrestrained rites of tellurian Aphrodite.

For Bachofen, matriarchal existence was a mode of life 'entirely subservient to matter and to the phenomena of natural life'. Its law was that all things come into being and pass away again in a never-ending cycle. Although it was true that 'the matriarchal peoples feel the unity of all life, the harmony of the universe',[25] this unity was one in which men (as opposed to women) found no satisfaction. The woman could, in the family she founded, achieve an existence which remained after her death. But men, having no lineage, were condemned to a transient and purely individual existence. They lived in obscurity and died leaving no trace.

This inconvenience found its remedy in the patriarchal system. What nature denies the law may affirm. If the primacy of woman is established by nature, that of man is founded on law. With the introduction of civil law as the rule of private and public life, the original unity of men with nature was replaced by the diversity of a truly political existence, in which, Bachofen claims, men might achieve 'the immortality of a supramaterial life'. As he puts it: 'The progress from material existence to a higher spiritual life coincides with progress from the one to the many, from the chaotic conditions to articulation. The human race begins with unity and material existence; multiplicity and higher spiritual existence are its goal. . . .'[26] Such, then, was the progress of the Spirit with reference to which all ancient mythology was to be understood.

Now, it is Bachofen's claim that what actually happened cannot, in itself, be the object of historical enquiry. What happened is merely the manifestation of what was thought, or more precisely, of the Spirit at that particular stage in its development; and it is the Spirit which is simultaneously the object and the subject of history. What is said and what is done are, therefore, to be treated as one and the same. 'Historical events provide the content, religion the form and expression. . . . One and the same myth encompasses religious and historical facts, and the two are not separate but identical.'[27] To take myths as evidence for what actually happened, as does the Euhemerist, is to take what is done as the reality and what is said as the appearance. In fact, both are equally appearances, and the reality they make manifest is the Spirit.

It is in the light of this consideration that we must interpret Bachofen's apparent Euhemerism. He tells us that 'All the myths relating to our subject embody a memory of real events experienced by the human race. They represent not fictions but historical realities.'[28] By this he does not mean that myths preserve the memory of actual historical events. He means that they preserve the religious significance of these events. The actual content of a myth, the specific events it narrates, may easily be complete fiction without the historical value of the myth being impaired. 'To deny the historicity of a legend does not divest it of value. What cannot have happened was nonetheless thought. External truth is replaced by inner truth. Instead of facts we find actions of the Spirit.'[29]

In myths, then, we find expressed the spiritual or religious experience of people. This being so, it matters little whether the events narrated are fact or fiction. Their true meaning is, in the last analysis, spiritual. But since it is the Spirit which is the determining factor in historical change, myths are also, in a sense, records of historical fact. The allegorical and the Euhemerist theories of myth are thus neatly reconciled.

Bachofen's theory is not a theory about myths as such. It is an explanation of myths in terms of a general theory about cultural formations and the changes they undergo; and, in this respect, it is undoubtedly an advance over the classical theories it was intended to supersede. However, as Engels remarked, the notion of a universal Spirit, the self-moving activities of which are sufficient to account for the whole of human history, 'must finally end in sheer mysticism'.[30] It makes possible a theory which is both all-embracing and irrefutable. We have merely to assume the existence of the Spirit and any human deed or utterance can then be seen as a manifestation of this Spirit in its march through history. There may be no positive grounds for rejecting the theory. But there are equally no good reasons for accepting it. We either believe in the Spirit or we do not.

It is, however, worth asking whether an Idealist theory, such as that of Bachofen, throws any real light on the meaning of a myth. A myth is an utterance made at a particular time and place. It has a meaning and this meaning is determined by its context. That is to say, we can discover what a myth means only by informing ourselves about the climate of opinion that prevailed at the time of its utterance and by reconstructing the manner in which the myth-maker himself intended his words to be understood. The Idealist, however, complicates the matter by arguing that a myth has, in effect, two authors: the myth-maker himself and the Spirit. The Spirit, being disembodied, requires a material spokesman through whom it can make its views known, and it finds such a spokesman in the individual myth-maker. The myth-maker himself is unaware of this arrangement, and the meanings he ascribes to his utterances are therefore not always the meanings intended by their true author, the Spirit. Indeed, the myth-maker may be left completely in the dark as to what it is he has actually said. Only the historian, looking back on the past from his vantage-point in the present, can see things in their true context, i.e. in the context of the Spirit's total enterprise.

It is, I think, clear that the Idealist historian is not concerned with the meaning (properly so called) of specific mythical utterances. He is concerned with their historical significance. He may well be right in supposing that the historical significance of what men say and do is apparent only in retrospect and that it attaches, not to what men intend, but to what they in actual fact achieve. But it is quite unnecessary to suggest that the historical significance of an utterance is the same thing as its meaning. Such a suggestion can, in any case, be sustained only by postulating a hypothetical, supra-individual entity endowed with all the traditional attributes of God. Bachofen's dictum that 'There is only one mighty lever of all civilization, and that is religion' is itself a statement of religious faith.

Bachofen is, perhaps, an extreme case. But the same confusion pervades the more cautious efforts of the modern allegorist. Myths, Bultmann tells us, should not be read literally. Their 'real purpose' is, not 'to present an objective picture of the world as it is', but to express 'man's understanding of his own existence'.[31] And this understanding may remain valid, even if the imagery in which it is expressed becomes obsolete. In a sense, of course, Bultmann is quite right. A myth may imply all sorts of general attitudes and preconceptions which the myth-maker himself takes for granted and which, therefore, hardly enter his mind. He takes them for granted because they form part of the climate of opinion or 'understanding of existence' within which he works; and, if we are to understand what he says, we must certainly familiarize ourselves with this climate of opinion. But we must not elevate it into a doctrine which we then declare to be the true meaning of the myth. This would be simply another way of asserting that, in his myths, it is not the myth-maker who speaks but the Spirit of his times. The myth-maker may well supply evidence from which later historians can infer the prevailing climate of opinion. But it is not his purpose to do so. His purpose is to make a specific point of some practical importance to his contemporaries. And it is this practical point that constitutes the *meaning*, as opposed to the historical significance, of what he says.

Linguistic, aetiological and ritual theories of myth

From time to time, both allegorists and Euhemerists had supported their interpretations by concocting etymologies for the names of the gods. It was an old technique the abuses of which Plato had exposed in his *Cratylus*. However, with the development of comparative linguistics in the nineteenth century the derivation of etymologies became an exact science; and the first to perceive the possibilities of this science was Max Müller, a trained philologist and Sanskrit scholar of international reputation.

According to Müller, the original Arygan tongue was, like all ancient languages, poor in abstract terms but rich in concrete and descriptive terms. It was, says Müller, 'simply impossible to speak of morning or evening, of spring and winter, without giving to these conceptions something of an individual, active, sexual, and at last, personal character'.[32] The most simple statement of fact tended to be couched in what we today would call poetic diction. 'Where we speak of the sun following the dawn, the ancient poets could only speak and think of the sun loving and embracing the dawn.'[33] And the Aryans, Müller suggested, were particularly given to making such unconsciously poetic pronouncements about natural phenomena, especially the daily movement of the sun across the heavens.

However, when the Aryan tribes dispersed, their language became more abstract and less poetic. The old poetry was preserved from one generation to the next, but, though the words in which it was expressed remained more or less the same, their meanings changed. This was largely due to the fact that, in the original Aryan tongue, objects tended to be called by their attributes, and, since most objects have many attributes, they had, during the early period of language, more than one name; and, on the other hand, where the same attribute attached to different objects, these objects tended to be called by the same name. Thus synonyms bred homonyms to produce a confusion which the later reduction of the language into a more rigidly systematic code was unable to eradicate. In time, the original names of the sun and other natural phenomena came to be understood as the proper names of gods and heroes; and simple descriptions of the sunrise and sunset were transformed into extravagant tales about Zeus and his consorts. Myth, in short, was nothing other than an ancient form of speech which, through a disease of language, had become incomprehensible to later and more prosaic generations.[34]

We cannot here trace the course of the long and acrimonious debate between Müller and his two chief critics, Tylor and Lang. In the case of certain ancient myths, Müller had undoubtedly established his point. However, as Lang pointed out, members of the philological school could not always agree where agreement was essential, namely, in their etymological analyses of mythical names. Furthermore, Müller's case suffered from his tendency to find in all myths, however disparate, a single theme: the rising and setting of the sun and the daily conflict between light and darkness. Finally, the fact that his method relied heavily on reducing Greek names to their Sanskrit roots raised the question as to whether his theory could be applied also to the myths of non-Aryan peoples.[35]

But Müller's greatest handicap was the support he received from his less gifted disciples. Among these, G. W. Cox stood foremost. Unwilling or unable to follow Müller through the byways of Sanskrit philology, Cox trod the path of proof by analogy. By comparing myths with one another, he found countless similarities in structure and motif, and this, to his mind, could only mean that all myths were fundamentally concerned with one subject, the sun. Comparative mythology in the manner of Cox soon became an irresistible target for the academic wits of the age. It was clear that, with sufficient ingenuity, anything from the song of sixpence to the career of Napoleon could be proved a solar myth. Indeed, was not Müller himself said to have migrated, like the sun, from east to west, from Germany to England? Did not his worshippers declare that he shed light where before there was darkness? And was his very name not proof enough that he could be none other than the legendary miller who grinds his corn with the great, fiery mill-stone of the sun? The great comparative mythologist himself was a solar myth, the sorry consequence of a linguistic disease.[36]

Both Tylor and Lang were too cautious to ascribe a single origin to all myths, but they did feel able to name one factor as being dominant. As Tylor put it, 'When the attention of a man in the myth-making state of the intellect is drawn to any phenomenon or custom which has to him no obvious reason, he invents and tells a story to account for it, and even if he does not persuade himself that this is a real legend of his forefathers, the story-teller who hears it from him and repeats it is troubled with no such difficulty.'[37] Myths, in short, are stories which primitive men devise for the purposes of explanation. They are attempted answers to those questions which curiosity provokes among savages no less than among civilized men.

The thesis was not entirely new. In his *De l'Origine des Fables* (1724), Fontenelle had argued that myths are merely the philosophy or science of primitive men. However, he had also maintained that the principles on which the savage proceeds are essentially no different from those that govern the activity of the modern philosopher.[38] And this Tylor and Lang were unable to accept. In their view, mythical explanations are the product of an intellectual state peculiar to the childlike mentality of savage peoples; and this intellectual state, they maintained, is characterized by a 'nebulous and confused frame of mind to which all things, animate or inanimate, human, animal, vegetable, or inorganic, seem on the same level of life, passion, and reason'.[39] In other words, the mark of the savage mind is that it cannot distinguish between what is human and what is merely natural. All departments of nature are equally endowed with life and personality. And, as Tylor argued, it is this belief in the animation of all nature, rising at its highest pitch to personification, which transfigures into myths the facts of daily experience.[40]

Although the theory maintained by Müller was more sophisticated than that of Tylor and Lang, it proved in the end to be less influential. By the turn of the century, the aetiological theory had won the day. Its victory was, however, short-lived, for it soon became apparent that, despite its merits, the theory suffered from a damaging defect, namely, its excessively intellectualist bias. The aetiologists had worked on the assumption that myths are a mass of ideas and that ideas are the fruit of a calm and contemplative mood. 'The savage,' Lang declared, 'is curious. The first faint impulses of the scientific spirit are at work in his brain; he is anxious to give himself an account of the world in which he finds himself.'[41] However, already in Lang's own time, a more pragmatic approach to myths had begun to make its mark. It was argued that, though the savage may be anxious to explain the world in which he lives, this anxiety has its source, not in the first faint impulses of the scientific spirit, but in the imperative need to secure the necessities of life. Thinking, it was said, cannot be usefully considered in abstraction from the realm of practical and social affairs because it is instrumental within that realm. Men think in order to act more effectively, and their thinking must therefore be understood as an integral part of their practical activities. In the study of myth, this view first found expression in the thesis that myths have their origin in ritual, a suggestion which gained prominence with the publication of Jane Harrison's *Themis* (1912).

A myth, according to Jane Harrison, is 'the spoken correlative of the acted rite, the thing done; it is *to legomenon* as contrasted with or rather as related to *to dromenon*'.[42] A rite, she tells us, is 'a thing done under strong emotional excitement, and done collectively'. High emotional tension is released through excited movement, and it is best expressed and maintained if the movement is collective and rhythmical, as in a dance.[43] Indeed, it is in the ritual dance that the savage feels most fully his unity with the group of which he is a member and with the natural world of which he is a part. Belief in the animation of all nature does not arise as a premiss in the reflections of primitive philosophers. It first emerges as an emotion experienced in the course of a ritual dance.

This collective emotion and feeling of unity with the world finds its outlet, not only in ritual action, but also in verbal utterance; and it is thus that myths are born. A myth is, like the rite it accompanies, simply the expression of an emotion collectively felt.

When, for one reason or another, men find themselves emotionally at a distance from their ritual, the 'things said' do indeed come to be transformed into explanations or justifications of the 'things done'. But, initially, a myth is not aetiological. 'Its object is not at first to give a reason; that notion is part of the old rationalist fallacy that saw in primitive man the leisured and eager enquirer bent on research.'[44] In its origin, a myth is the verbal correlate of a ritual; and it is this ritual character that distinguishes a true myth from any other kind of narrative or traditional tale.

Jane Harrison herself tended to associate the origins of myths with the era of human culture when the Dionysiac spirit and the laws of mother-right prevailed. The influence of Nietzsche and Bachofen is apparent throughout her work. But later advocates of the theory dispensed with these intriguing associations and emphasized instead the practical aspects of myth-making. Ritual, they argued, is essentially a primitive form of sympathetic magic. It is a collective attempt to influence the course of nature and thus to secure the necessities of life: health, food, children and so forth. And myth has much the same purpose. Being an integral part of a ritual performance, a myth expresses the collective will of the group on some matter of immediate practical concern; and its recitation is normally accompanied by the high emotional excitement that occurs whenever the individual sinks his identity into that of the group to which he belongs.[45]

In its extreme form, the theory claims a ritual origin for all myths whatsoever; and this is obviously unsatisfactory. The number of known myths is enormous and it is only in a few cases that we have any evidence concerning the circumstances in which they were formed. There is no doubt that some myths did originate in rituals. But it is equally certain that others did not. And as for the rest, where the evidence is insufficient or altogether lacking, the question of their origin cannot be answered and should, therefore, not be asked. Certainly, the origins of myths should never be deduced *a priori*. Lord Raglan rightly remarks that most students of mythology accept that 'there is in some cases a connection between myth and ritual', but his suggestion that we should therefore apply 'the simple scientific principle that similar causes produce similar effects' is thoroughly misleading.[46] To admit a connection is not the same as to admit a causal relationship. And, in any case, there is nothing scientific about the argument that, because some myths have a ritual origin, all myths have a ritual origin. It is merely one of the more obvious logical fallacies.

These defects lie on the surface, and the advocates of the ritual theory have been among the first to detect them. Many of them have, therefore, adopted a modified version of the theory. They point out that, when all is said and done, we are left with the fact that many myths are, in practice, connected with rituals. We may not be able to say much about the origin of myths in general, or even of these myths in particular; but we can say that myth and ritual, when found together, are consubstantial, that is, that they are one thing viewed from different angles.[47] As Kluckhohn puts it: 'The myth is a system of word symbols, whereas ritual is a system of object and act symbols. Both are symbolic processes for dealing with the same type of situation in the same affective mode.' They occur together because they both 'satisfy a group of identical or closely related needs of individuals'.[48]

So far as political myths are concerned, this suggestion offers a promising line of enquiry. Several commentators have observed that, in totalitarian societies, political myths and political rituals go hand in hand. Any sudden disintegration of the established order, whether through revolution or economic collapse, breeds the need for a new understanding of man's place in the world and for new ways of going about the ordinary business of life, and this need is satisfied by the introduction of new myths and new rituals. In the myths, the nation's past is dramatized in such a way as to make its future destiny apparent; and, in the rituals, obsolete customs are replaced by gestures and ceremonies which sustain the uncertain solidarity of the people and illustrate their new-found conception of what they are about. The myths and the rituals are, thus, distinct but related aspects of the same enterprise.[49]

However, the example of totalitarian states should not tempt us into too ready an acceptance of the ritual theory. Political myths and political rituals are by no means confined to totalitarian states. Indeed, they may occur in any society sophisticated enough to boast a political culture; and, as often as not, their relationship with one another is anything but clear. Many political myths (e.g. the Myth of the Norman Yoke) are not accompanied by any significant body of ritual; and many political rituals (e.g. presidential inauguration ceremonies) have nothing directly to do with any known myth. And even where there happens to be a close and obvious relationship, such as in the American Independence Day celebrations, it is usually the myth that gives rise to the ritual, not the ritual that gives rise to the myth.

Myth as a primitive world-view

The theorist who, more than any other, has drawn attention to the use of myths in contemporary politics is Ernst Cassirer. Indeed, as a study of political myths, his *The Myth of the State* has yet to be superseded. However, his earlier and more important work, *The Philosophy of Symbolic Forms*, displays no direct preoccupation with political affairs. Here his intention is to investigate 'mythical consciousness' as such or, rather, to develop 'the phenomenology of myth'. Myth, to his mind, is a coherent and self-sufficient world of symbolic forms. It is a *Weltauschauung* that he finds expressed, not only in sacred tales, but also in totemic practices, magic, astrology and ritual; and it comprises a total approach to experience which, he suggests, is characteristic only of very ancient or very primitive cultures. He accordingly develops his analysis of mythical consciousness by contrasting it with the empirical or scientific consciousness of modern man.

Empirical thought, he tells us, begins where consciousness first makes a clear distinction between illusion and fact, between the merely subjective and the objective. We do not take a particular sense impression for what it is in its immediacy. Instead, we compare it critically with other sense impressions in order to establish whether it is confirmed by experience as a whole. We distinguish the transient from the permanent, the variable from the constant and the accidental from the necessary and thus, Cassirer maintains, we acquire a world of objective and determinate reality as against a world of mere representation or imagination.[50]

The mythical thinker also regards the contents of his thought as constituting a world of reality. But (Cassirer maintains) his relation to this world 'discloses no sign of that decisive "crisis" with which empirical and conceptual knowledge begin'.[51] Primitive man cannot, as we do, withdraw from the presence of phenomena. What he perceives he perceives in its immediacy as something unique and, above all, as something endowed with vital force or personality. Being completely absorbed in the immediacy of his experience, he cannot differentiate between reality and appearance. 'Whatever is capable of affecting mind, feeling, or will has thereby established its undoubted reality.'[52] The objects of his dreams and fantasies are, consequently, no less real than the objects of his senses.

In mythical consciousness, then, everything appears as a concrete, individual Thou. This includes, not only objects, but also their parts, their attributes, the changes they undergo and the feelings they evoke. Death, for instance, is an individual substance endowed with a will and a personality of its own. The same holds for attributes and capacities (such as light, strength or fertility) and for feelings such as fear and hope. All are equally experienced as real, living substances. It is inevitable, therefore, that mythical consciousness should be unable to distinguish between the symbol and the thing symbolized. In so far as the symbolic representation of a thing evokes the same feelings as the thing itself, it is taken to be identical with the thing. The symbol and what it signifies coalesce. In myth, Cassirer maintains, nothing is represented by something else. The image *is* the thing, not a representation of the thing.[53]

By the same token, there is, in myth, a marked tendency to identify the part with the whole. The whole man, for instance, may be contained in his hair, his nail-cuttings, his clothes or his footprints because they are each felt to be pregnant with the full significance of the man. 'Similarly, the genus,' Cassirer tells us, 'is not a universal which logically determines the particular but is immediately present, living and acting in this particular.'[54] Each individual embodies the species as a whole; and, *vice versa*, the species as a whole is credited with the attributes of any one of its particular members.

Having established all this, Cassirer goes on to elucidate the manner in which the notions of cause, space and time appear in mythical thought. Empirical science, he notes, determines the causes of a thing by isolating the necessary and sufficient conditions for its occurrence. The causes are, normally, both general and impersonal. But, while the scientist is content to apprehend an individual event as an instance of a general law, a general law cannot do justice to the individuality of the event, and it is precisely the individuality of events which primitive man experiences and to which he applies his imagination. His explanation of an event therefore takes the form of postulating individual acts of will. To borrow an example from Henri Frankfort: 'If the rivers refuse to rise, it is not suggested that the lack of rainfall on distant mountains adequately explains the calamity. When the river does not rise, it has *refused* to rise. The river, or the gods, must be angry with the people who depend on the inundation.'[55]

The same complete absorption in the immediacy of experience infects also the mythical awareness of space. 'Space is postulated by us to be infinite, continuous, and homogenous—attributes which mere sensual perception does not reveal. But primitive thought cannot abstract a concept "space" from its experience of space. ... The spatial concepts of the primitive are concrete orientations; they refer to localities which have an emotional colour.'[56] Primitive man, in short, does not experience space as such. He experiences only a number of different places each of which is a concrete individual thing. What distinguishes them is the fact that they have different associations and therefore evoke different feelings. Conversely, places which have the same associations and evoke the same feelings are taken to be the same place. In ancient Egypt, for example, there were a number of temples each centred upon an allegedly primeval mound on which the sun-god stood when he made the world. For the Egyptians, there was no difficulty in regarding all of these mounds as being, in reality, the same place.

The notion of time, in myth, falls into the same pattern as the notion of space. There is no question of primitive man abstracting a concept of time from his concrete experience of time. Time, as he experiences it, is a number of particular times each of which is endowed with its own peculiar qualities and significance. Childhood, adolescence, maturity and old age are such times; so are each of the four seasons, the phases of the moon and the other well-defined periods in the cycle of nature. And it goes without saying that times which have the same individual character are, by the primitive, regarded as being the same time. 'As we know, it lies in the essence of mythical thinking that wherever it posits a relation, it causes the members of this relation to flow together and merge; and this rule of concrescence, this growing together of the members of a relation, prevails also in the mythical consciousness of time.'[57]

This, however, does not mean that myth is a totally incoherent realm of experience. Though the mythical thinker may dispense with the distinction between reality and appearance, he does so only because he has a serviceable substitute at hand. In mythical thought, Cassirer tells us, 'All reality and all events are projected into the fundamental opposition of the sacred and the profane.' It is true that the character of being sacred does not, from the very outset, belong to specific objects. Indeed, anything, however commonplace, 'can suddenly participate in it'. It has merely to 'fall under the specific mythical-religious perspective' and it thereby becomes sacred. And all things thus sanctified 'form a self-enclosed realm and possess a common tonality, by which they are distinguished from the contents of common, everyday, empirical existence'.[58]

In his *Philosophy of Symbolic Forms*, then, Cassirer argues that myth is the world-view of pre-scientific societies and that it cannot coexist with the empirical *Weltanschauung* of modern man. It is a view which, in one form or another, was shared by most of Cassirer's predecessors and which has since found expression in the work of his many disciples.

Gunnell and Frankfort, for instance, tell us that the mythic *Weltan-schauung* of archaic societies is a world of experience in which time and change are 'sublimated in the concrete, recurrent, and spatially grounded rhythms of nature'. Only when the impact of historical change brings temporality into play is the all-embracing unity of the 'integral myth' dissolved to be replaced by other symbolic forms, such as history and philosophy. And politics (according to Gunnell) emerges as an attempt to combat the destructiveness of time through the establishment of an enduring social order based on authority. Politics is, in other words, a substitute for myth, a *pis aller* which man must endure as a penalty for his 'fall into time'.[59]

It is a fascinating thesis; but it would be far more persuasive if it did not rest on so obvious an academic sleight of hand. What Gunnell and Frankfort have done is to select certain isolated features of archaic cultures, erect them into a systematic world-view, and then claim that this world-view encompasses the entire experience of archaic man. This is, quite simply, bad history. There are, certainly, societies in which myths are more common than they are in ours; and it is true that philosophy and science now occupy much of the ground that once belonged to myths. But there never has been a society the members of which understood the world *entirely* in terms of either myth or science; nor will there ever be such a society. In *The Myth of the State*, Cassirer himself acknowledges the point. Even in primitive societies, he tells us, myth does not pervade the whole of man's conscious life. In their normal everyday occupations, primitive men proceed in much the same pragmatic and empirical fashion as their civilized counterparts. It is only when faced with a task that seems beyond their natural powers that they resort to myths and magic. And this, Cassirer adds, applies also to the highly civilized societies of Western Europe.[60]

None the less, Cassirer retains his view that there is something irreducibly primitive about the use of myths. Civilized men, he believes, conduct their affairs according to the principles of reason, and the intrusion of myth into contemporary politics is not only unwelcome but somehow anomalous. 'Scientific knowledge and technical mastery of nature daily win new and unprecedented victories. But in man's practical and social life the defeat of rational thought seems to be complete and irrevocable. In this domain modern man is supposed to forget everything he has learned in the development of his intellectual life. He is admonished to go back to the first rudimentary stages of human culture.'[61]

It is difficult to see what grounds Cassirer has for taking this view. His suggestion that modern men conduct their political affairs using methods analogous to those of science and technology is untenable and is probably not what he really means. As for the supposedly primitive character of myth, there is, as Cassirer himself admits, as great a difference between the myths of our time and those of primitive societies as there is between a modern town house and a mud hut.[62] Myth-making is characteristic of culture as such and is no more a reversion to 'the first rudimentary stages of human culture' than are dancing, painting and architecture.

There is a further objection. Cassirer insists that all myths are, by definition, concerned with the intrusion of the sacred into an otherwise secular world; and, indeed, he sees in the modern totalitarian myth-maker 'the priest of a new, entirely irrational and mysterious religion'.[63] But, in fact, there are many myths in which the sacred plays no role whatsoever, and most modern political myths, including those of which Cassirer speaks, fall into this category. They do, indeed, inspire their devotees with a high degree of enthusiasm but enthusiasm can occur without any notion of the sacred being involved and is therefore not the same as religion. The view that myth is a form of religion can in the end result only in one of two things. We must either take a strong stand on the definition and stoutly deny that certain well-known myths are myths; or we must abandon ourselves to a course of remarkably tortuous and obscurantist interpretations. It is, I think, far simpler to say that, while the distinction between the sacred and the profane may (as Durkheim says) give us the minimum definition of religion, it is by no means a necessary feature of mythical thought. No doubt, many religious ideas are to be found in myths, especially in the myths of primitive societies; but it is not the case that all myths contain religious ideas or that we have any good reason to regard myth as a kind of religion.

This, however, does not mean that the events and situations described in a myth have no special significance which sets them apart from the realm of everyday affairs. The myth-maker may not see things in a distinctively religious light, but he does have a standpoint which gives him a perspective different from that of Cassirer's empirical thinker. He orders his experience on the assumption that the present is an episode in a story, an incident in a dramatic development; and it is this (I suggest) that enables him to distinguish between what is significant and what is not. Any person, thing, place, time or event has significance in so far as the myth-maker can fit it into his plot. Depending on the myth to which he subscribes, he will see a particular tract of land as part of the territory from which the chosen people were expelled, a particular year as the one in which Christ will establish his kingdom on earth, a particular trade-unionist as an agent of the worldwide Communist conspiracy, or a particular industrial dispute as a crucial incident in the class war. And whatever is thus incorporated into his account acquires thereby a significance and a 'reality' that other things lack.

Although we must reject Cassirer's main thesis, much of what he says concerning the nature of mythical thinking still holds good. As we shall see, there is unquestionably a sense in which the myth-maker confuses the part with the whole and regards persons and situations with the same characteristics as being substantially the same. Cassirer is not the first to draw attention to these points; but he is the first to give them systematic treatment, and herein lies the merit of his work. However, his early view that myth is some kind of pre-scientific *Weltanschauung* leads him to complicate and mystify matters which prove, on inspection, to be perfectly straightforward.

The question of origins

Many of the theories we have discussed seek to establish the meanings and purposes of myths, not by taking them in their contemporary context, but by harking back to their origins. This quest after the origins of things owes at least part of its appeal to the belief that, if we could only discover what a thing was when it first began, we would have the explanation of its true character. According to this view, the world as we know it is a world of mere appearances or manifestations. In itself, it is a puzzling and unsatisfactory world which, if it is to be understood at all, must be understood in terms of something other than itself. It must be understood in terms of the reality which lies behind the appearances and which somehow determines them; and this reality is surely none other than the world as it was at its origin. As Bachofen put it, 'It is the origins which determine the subsequent development, which define its character and direction.'[64]

Although this is an attractive view, its application to the study of myths has proved less successful than we might expect. Let us begin with the suggestion that the manifest content of a myth is not its true content. Myths, it is argued, appear to be ridiculous stories about gods and heroes but, in fact, they are descriptions of natural phenomena, historical events or ritual performances. This discrepancy between the real and the apparent content of a myth is due to the distortions that occur when an account is handed down from one generation to the next. This seems reasonable enough. The content of a myth can certainly change in the course of time, giving us different successive versions of the same story; and it is plausible to postulate an *urmythos*, an original myth of which all subsequent versions are the degenerate offspring. But what can this *urmythos* tell us about the content of its successors? It might, of course, make us better able to say in what respects the myth has changed; but, in itself, it will not explain these changes. The original contents of a myth serve only as the inert material which, for one reason or another, is elaborated and recast. A myth does not shape itself. It is shaped and reshaped by the men who pass it on; and they shape it in accordance with their own presuppositions and in response to their particular experience of the world. So far as the content of a myth is concerned, it is not its origin which defines its character and direction. And there is no significant sense in which the content of the first version is more 'real' than that of any subsequent version.

The same considerations apply when we turn to the meaning or message which a myth conveys. A myth, it will be said, has a true meaning, namely, the one intended by its originator; and this meaning is somehow implicit in all subsequent versions of the myth, although those who transmit it may not be aware of the fact. It is not difficult to see what is wrong with this suggestion. No myth has a true meaning or meaning in itself apart from the meaning it has for those who tell it. Old myths are not kept in circulation merely (as Müller supposed) because man 'has an inborn reverence for the past'.[65] They are kept in circulation because they convey something of interest and significance to the teller and his audience. Whatever this something may be, it cannot be hidden or implicit. A myth means what it is consciously intended or understood to mean by those among whom it circulates. The meaning a myth has on the first occasion of its being told is, therefore, in no way privileged. It is a meaning like any other, and chances are that a change in circumstances will render it obsolete and bring a new and more appropriate meaning to the fore. The old meaning does not remain implicit in the new version of the myth. It is simply discarded like any other useless article.

It might be argued that myths are intended to convey timeless truths so profound and so remote from ordinary experience that they cannot be expressed directly and that, for all their differences in detail, the various versions of a myth are fundamentally driving at the same point and have a single meaning. We will have to return to this suggestion at a later stage, but for the moment, we note that, even if it were valid, it would not strengthen the argument that the true meaning of a myth is the one intended by the man who told it first. If a myth is a timeless truth ambiguously expressed, then this holds as much for the first version as it does for the last. There is no reason to suppose that the first narrator, merely because he was the first, possessed greater insight or powers of expression than his successors.

The suggestion offered by the ritual theorists, that it is the practical purpose of a myth that stands revealed at its origin, need not detain us long. A myth may well be used for one purpose at one time and for a different purpose at another. But it does not follow that one of the two purposes must therefore be bogus. Both are equally 'real'. Like its meaning, the purpose of a myth depends entirely on the circumstances in which it is told and on the intentions of the man who tells it. It does not depend on the manner in which the myth originates.

This is not to deny that the search for the origins of myths is an interesting and valuable pursuit. But, interesting as it is, it must not be confused with the quite separate enquiry into the meanings and purposes of myths. Nor must we be seduced by the view that things are somehow more real at their origin. They are not more real; they are merely different.

Chapter Two

Psychological theories of myth

I have voiced doubts about the thesis that myths have a life of their own and that their meanings and purposes can be established in abstraction from their particular historical context. At the risk of being tedious, I shall pursue this point a bit further, for it lies at the heart of many theories which nowadays dominate the study of political myths. Of these, the most common is the view that a myth is primarily a psychological phenomenon. Tucker, for instance, argues that Marx's vision of the class struggle is nothing but a projection upon the outside world of a psychological conflict which actually took place within Marx himself; and 'this is the decisive characteristic of mythic thought, that something by nature interior is apprehended as exterior, that a drama of the inner life of man is experienced and depicted as taking place in the outer world'.[1] Similarly, Norman Cohn sees in the millennialist movements of the Middle Ages the projection of a paranoia that has its source, ultimately, in the breakdown of trust between father and son.[2] Interpretations such as these owe their general inspiration to the work of Freud and Jung and their particular methodological assumptions to the Freudian theory of dreams.

A dream, Freud tells us, is 'a performance and an utterance on the part of the dreamer, but of a kind that conveys nothing to us, and which we do not understand'.[3] The dream, however, is not meaningless. Indeed, it has a hidden meaning; and this hidden meaning is to be found in the 'latent dream-thoughts' of which the 'manifest dream-content' is a distorted rendering. The distortion is necessary for, without it, the dream could not fulfil its function.

Dreams, Freud argues, are brought about by a wish, and their purpose is to represent the wish as being fulfilled, thus enabling the dreamer to continue his sleep undisturbed. Many dreams, especially those of young children, are quite plainly imaginary fulfilments of a wish that has not been satisfied in waking life. But most adult dreams are more complicated, the reason being that the wishes they fulfil are of a kind the dreamer himself would not care to acknowledge and has therefore 'repressed' or relegated to the unconscious. Many of these repressed wishes have, according to Freud, their source in the sexual experiences of early childhood. For example, the male child develops a strong sexual attachment to his mother and a corresponding desire to do away with his father. But, polite society being what it is, such desires must remain unsatisfied and, indeed, put completely out of mind. They are not, however, forgotten. They are relegated to the unconscious where they remain to plague the sleep of adult life.[4]

If sleep is to continue without interruption, these unconscious wishes, which the relaxation of consciousness brings to the surface, must be satisfied in some way or another; but, at the same time, the satisfaction cannot be directly or unambiguously represented, for this would so offend the decent values of the dreamer that his sleep would be troubled and the purpose of the dream frustrated. The dream is, in this sense, a compromise between conflicting desires. Hence its distorted and ambivalent character.[5]

The distorting 'dream-work' whereby the latent thoughts are translated into the manifest content of the dream takes many forms. First of all, the mere fact that a dream consists of visual images and symbols rather than verbal statements entails a certain amount of distortion. Secondly, a kind of 'censorship' takes place in that the distasteful elements in the latent thoughts are either omitted, modified or given an apparently unimportant place in the finished dream. Thirdly, there is the process Freud calls 'condensation'. Latent elements with a common characteristic can, in the final dream, be joined together so that one visual image expresses several latent thoughts. And, finally, the latent thoughts are further distorted by the process of 'secondary elaboration', the object of which is to combine the immediate results of the dream-work into 'a single and fairly coherent whole'.[6]

Freud himself never extended his theory of dreams to the study of myth. But he did observe that many of the symbols which appear in dreams occur also in myths, as do certain basic themes connected with infantile sexuality, the story of Oedipus being the most famous case in point. He also insisted that myths are like dreams in that they are products of 'fantasy'.[7] These suggestions were taken up and elaborated into a general theory partly by Otto Rank and, more explicitly, by Karl Abraham.[8]

Abraham's thesis is that what Freud said about dreams applies *in toto* to myths. A myth is a product of fantasy, and, in myths, we accordingly find repressed wishes represented as being fulfilled. It is true that, unlike dreams, myths do not originate in the emotions peculiar to any one individual. A myth is somehow a collective product. But there are emotions common to all men and these express themselves in what Freud called 'typical dreams'. According to Abraham, they also express themselves in myths. Furthermore, just as dreams reveal the repressed emotions, anxieties and wishes of the individual's childhood, so a myth is 'a fragment of the repressed life of the infantile psyche of the race'. In its myths, the human race experiences the fulfilment of its wishes. Indeed, he continues, in the 'childhood' of the race, 'when more natural relations still prevail, when the conventions have not yet assumed rigid forms, every tendency could be realized'. Later, these tendencies are supressed in a manner similar to the process of repression in the individual. But, like the repressed wishes of the individual, they do not die out altogether. They are retained in the myths of the race, just as, in the case of the individual, they are retained in his dreams. This process, for which Abraham coins the phrase 'mass repression', is 'the reason the people no longer understand the original meaning of their myths, quite as we can not understand our dreams without some explanation'.[9]

The sufficient objection to this view is that it is founded on a false analogy. The human race is not, in any relevant respect, similar to an individual. It has no father or mother; it cannot get depressed, neurotic or drunk; and, unlike the individuals of which it is composed, it has no sexual problems because it has no sex life. Above all, it does not go to sleep and have dreams. It might be argued that Abraham's remarks apply, not to the race as such, but to its individual members and that the wishes and anxieties which are revealed in a myth are personal wishes and anxieties which happen to be shared by a number of these individuals. But, if this is his argument, then clearly the repressed wishes which a myth reflects will have their source, not in 'the childhood of the race', but in the childhoods of the individuals concerned. In any case, the human race does not (except in a metaphorical sense) have a childhood. What we know of ancient and primitive peoples does not suggest that their social relations are any more 'natural' than those which prevail in civilized societies. Nor are there any grounds for supposing that a primitive adult is any more infantile than his civilized counterpart. He may be technologically less advanced, but that is a different matter.

Furthermore, Freud himself stressed those very aspects of his theory which make it inapplicable to anything else but dreams. The object of dreams, he tells us, is not to communicate anything; 'on the contrary, it is important to them not to be understood'.[10] It may be that the purpose of interpretation is to turn the dream into a normal communication, but the fact remains that the dream itself is a purely private hallucination which serves the particular purpose of allowing the dreamer to continue his sleep undisturbed. A myth, on the other hand, is everything a dream is not. It is pre-eminently a public rather than a private utterance; it is one of the oldest and most effective ways men have devised for making themselves understood; and its purpose, whatever else it might be, has nothing to do with enabling men to get a good night's sleep.

It is, in fact, misleading to describe myths as the spontaneous products of fantasy. To be sure, a myth does not deal in generalities. It is a story and must therefore consist of statements about concrete events and particular persons or groups of persons. It evokes, in the first instance, pictures or images rather than abstract concepts. But, although a myth is not a piece of abstract thinking, it is none the less a carefully contrived and disciplined statement. A myth is a story and there is nothing confused or haphazard about a story. The story-teller must include all that is necessary to his purpose and eliminate all that is irrelevant. Every episode in his narrative (except the first and the last) must, in some sense, follow from the preceding episode and help prepare the ground for the conclusion. The thinking involved may not be what a philosopher would regard as logical, but it is systematic thinking nevertheless. Myths, therefore, can not be represented as the work of unfettered fantasy, and this is what differentiates them from dreams: dreams, taken as they stand, are meaningless, but myths are coherent and meaningful statements in their own right. And to suggest that myths should be read as garbled accounts of what happens in the myth-maker's unconscious mind is to miss the point. Myths are not stories about the unconscious. They are what they seem to be, namely, stories about the material world in which the myth-maker finds himself.

Like Freud, Jung finds, in the typical motifs of dreams and myths, a symbolic significance which, in his view, can have its source only in the unconscious. And, to this extent, his theory lies open to the objections I have just mentioned. However, his notion of the unconscious differs from that of Freud in one important respect. Freud insists that, however typical they may be, the contents of the unconscious are ultimately personal in character because they are always derived from something that happened in the individual's own conscious experience. This view is, according to Jung, untenable. It cannot account for the fact that certain mythological motifs occur in the dreams of individuals who could not possibly have got them from the culture in which they live. Jung allows that cross-fertilization has made most cultures astonishingly rich in content; and he takes the point that men generally relegate to the unconscious and thus 'forget' much of what they pick up in daily conversation. But, he claims, when all such factors have been accounted for, we are still left with individuals who display, in their dreams and fantasies, a mythological knowledge which cannot be traced to any source in their conscious experience.[11]

It is this consideration that leads Jung to propose his theory of the collective unconscious. As he puts it: 'A more or less superficial layer of the unconscious is undoubtedly personal. I call it the *personal unconscious*. But this personal unconscious rests upon a deeper layer, which does not derive from personal experience and is not a personal acquisition but is inborn. This deeper layer I call the *collective unconscious*. I have chosen the term "collective" because this part of the unconscious is not individual but universal; in contrast to the personal psyche, it has contents and modes of behaviour that are more or less the same everywhere and in all individuals. It is, in other words, identical in all men and thus constitutes a common psychic substrate of a suprapersonal nature which is present in every one of us.'[12] The contents of the collective unconscious are, in Jung's work, termed archetypes. He often speaks of these archetypes as 'universal images that have existed since the remotest times' and compares them with Plato's intelligible Forms.[13] It is, however, not his intention to revive the bankrupt theory of innate ideas. His point is that, since each individual is born 'with a differentiated brain that is predetermined by heredity', the brain 'meets sensory stimuli coming from outside, not with *any* aptitudes', but with specific 'instincts and preformed patterns'. In other words, 'It is not, therefore, a question of inherited *ideas* but of inherited *possibilities* of ideas.'[14] The archetype itself, then, has no positive content. It is a mere potentiality; and this carries the important implication that it never appears in consciousness and can not, therefore, be observed. It can be known only through its effects, that is, through the various concrete images or 'archetypal ideas' in which it manifests itself. Dreams and myths, in short, are composed, not of archetypes, but of images which represent or symbolize the archetypes.

It is, according to Jung, the purpose of dreams, myths and other forms of fantasy to bring into the awareness of the individual the drama that is enacted deep within his psyche. The collective unconscious accomplishes this by appropriating concrete objects and events and using them as a symbolic language in which it can make statements about itself. This appropriation is not entirely arbitrary. Indeed, it is determined by the manner in which the archetypes themselves were formed. The archetypes are, Jung tells us, 'deposits of the constantly repeated experiences of humanity', which endless repetition has engraved into our psychic constitution in the form of predispositions or potentialities.[15] When a situation occurs which corresponds to a given archetype, that archetype is activated and appropriates the situation as a mirror-image or symbol of itself. And this process of appropriation is, Jung tells us, particularly conspicuous among primitive people. 'It is not enough for the primitive to see the sun rise and set; this external observation must at the same time be a psychic happening: the sun in its course must represent the fate of a god or hero who, in the last analysis, dwells nowhere except in the soul of man. All the mythological processes of nature ... are symbolic expressions of the inner, unconscious drama of the psyche which becomes accessible to man's consciousness by way of projection—that is, mirrored in the events of nature.'[16] In other words, although he is not aware of the fact, the primitive projects onto the world around him events that actually take place deep within his unconscious self. And thus external events become archetypal ideas and acquire their peculiar 'mythical' significance.

The purpose of this process is to secure the effective unity of the individual's personality. Primitive man, according to Jung, differs from his civilized counterpart in that his conscious life is dominated to a far greater degree by the activities of his collective unconscious. Everywhere, the archetypes impose themselves on his waking thoughts. Indeed, it is not so much the individual who thinks as his unconscious self. However, as consciousness extends its scope, it appears to improve its control over the life of the individual. The unconscious becomes, so to speak, dissociated from the individual's conscious life. And this, Jung argues, brings about a dangerous situation, for the unconscious is not thereby rendered inactive. On the contrary, it remains a powerful and active force in the personality of the individual. But, since it finds no place in his conscious experience, it is no longer subject to his control. His personality loses its unity, and he becomes liable to 'psychic epidemics' in which the archetypes burst into consciousness with results that vary from individual psychosis to mass hysteria. 'There is,' Jung remarks, 'no lunacy people under the domination of an archetype will not fall prey to. If thirty years ago anyone had dared to predict that our psychological development was tending towards a revival of the medieval persecutions of the Jews, that Europe would again tremble before the Roman fasces and the tramp of legions, that people would once more give the Roman salute, as two thousand years ago, and that instead of the Christian cross an archaic swastika would lure onwards millions of warriors ready for death—why, that man would have been hooted at as a mystical fool. And today? Surprising as it may seem, all this absurdity is a horrible reality.'[17]

Jung's argument is certainly one way to account for the hypnotic power a political myth-maker often wields. But this must not blind us to its many shortcomings as a theory. It is, to begin with, not a theory specifically about myths. Archetypal ideas can, in Jung's view, occur in any product of the imagination, whether it be a dream, a poem, an alchemical treatise or an essay in religious mysticism. A myth is none of these, and we have not accounted for myths when we have explained the nature of archetypal ideas. Furthermore, the independence Jung ascribes to the workings of the collective unconscious places his theory firmly in the Idealist tradition. Indeed, he himself acknowledges this.[18] The supra-individual Spirit which governs our merely individual activities now wreaks its havoc from a safe refuge deep in the unconscious psyche; but it is recognizably the same Spirit that once haunted the pages of Hegel and Bachofen, and, although transformed, it remains an unsubstantiated hypothesis. The universal diffusion of certain mythological motifs is no doubt an interesting fact, but, in itself, it no more proves the existence of the collective unconscious than the balance of nature proves the existence of God. To explain a set of facts by postulating a hypothetical cause and then citing as evidence for the existence of this cause the very facts we set out to explain is not, as Jung supposes, science; it is, at best, intelligent guess-work.

Finally, both Freud and Jung make the same methodological error that brought comparative mythology into disrepute at the end of the last century. Noticing that many of the motifs and images found in dreams occur also in myths they argue that, because a given motif has a certain meaning in the context of a dream, it therefore has the same meaning in the quite different context of a myth. Just as the comparative mythologist might cheerfully identify any circular object with the sun, so Freud, with equal abandon, reduces them all to the female sex organ. This simply will not do. We cannot come to myths with a preconceived idea of the symbolic significance of certain images and then claim that this significance constitutes the 'hidden meaning' of the myths.[19]

Nothing I have said should be taken to deny that myths often have profound psychological effects on men, or that men sometimes seek to alleviate their personal anxieties by adopting a mythical point of view. Nor need we deny that myths (particularly eschatological myths) depict the imaginary satisfaction of unfulfilled wishes. But these wishes and anxieties often stem, neither from the childhood tribulations nor from the collective unconscious of the individuals concerned, but from the real and present prospect of persecution, war, starvation or frustrated ambition.

Sociological theories of myth

Despite their protests to the contrary, Freud and Jung tended to see all myths as the product of a single cause, namely, the operations of the unconscious. Many social scientists reject this view, not (as they should) because it is reductionist, but because it is reductionist in the wrong direction. Myths, they will say, are not manifestations of the unconscious; they are the collective achievement of the social group to which the myth-maker belongs. 'In mythical thought and imagination,' Cassirer declares, 'we do not meet with *individual* confessions. Myth is an objectification of man's social experience, not of his individual experience.' It is true that myths are sometimes concocted by individuals. Plato's myths are a case in point. But we cannot count such fictions as being genuine myths. 'Plato created them in an entirely free spirit; he was not under their power, he directed them according to his own purposes.'[20]

Cassirer is here recalling the view, advanced by Levy-Bruhl and Durkheim, that myths are collective representations. Collective representations, it seems, include all doctrines, ideas and concepts shared by the members of a given social group. Their definitive mark is their impersonal character. They bear the stamp of no individual mind. They are not invented by the individual but are, like the language in which they are expressed, imposed on him, and he comes to share in the possession of them by learning to converse with his fellows. He may, by his critical efforts, modify them; but, even so, they remain the collective product of the group to which he belongs. They existed before him, and, when he dies, they will survive him.[21]

Durkheim often talks as if a society has a collective mind which thinks independently of the thinking done by its individual members.[22] This is, of course, nonsense. A society is not the sort of thing that can think. Thinking is an activity performed only by individuals. We may grant that the total mass of concepts, like the language in which they are expressed, is not the product of any single individual. But then a mere mass of concepts is not a thought or even a collection of thoughts. A thought is a construct, and the constructing has to be done by an individual. Concepts are, so to speak, the materials out of which thoughts are made. In much the same way, a language is not a statement or a collection of statements, but a code in which statements can be communicated.

This brings us to our point. A myth certainly seems to be a collective representation in the broad sense defined by Levy-Bruhl and Durkheim. It is, typically, the shared possession of the community in which it is current, and it is not thought of as being the invention of any particular individual. Individual members of the community find it already in existence, and they draw upon it for a variety of purposes. But, in itself, it is not, and cannot be, an act of communication. When an individual makes use of a myth, he states, not the myth, but a particular version of it. He elaborates or modifies the myth to suit the needs of the moment. He may follow an established myth as closely as he pleases; but, since it is always in a particular time and place that he speaks, he cannot avoid shaping his account to fit the circumstances. A given myth, in other words, finds expression in a number of mythical accounts. And, indeed, it is only by examining many versions or mythical accounts that the historian can gather what the myths of a society are, for a myth has no determinate existence apart from the different versions of it put forward in argument by various interested individuals.

The failure to distinguish between myths and the particular instances of their use has, I believe, caused much unnecessary confusion. When mythologists speak of a myth, they usually mean the myth in abstraction from the various mythical accounts in which it is expressed. And this has led them to see the myth, not as a collection of thematically similar arguments, but as some kind of transcendent reality. There would be nothing wrong with this, were it not for the fact that, concerning myths thus reified, there is virtually nothing sensible to be said. The Myth of the Norman Yoke, for instance, explains nothing and makes no prescriptions. If asked what the myth means, we would have to reply that it meant one thing to some people and another thing to others. And we would have to give a similar answer if asked to explain its purpose. However, we find ourselves in a markedly more satisfactory position when we consider, not the Myth of the Norman Yoke, but a particular version of it, such as that contained in the Diggers' *Appeal to the House of Commons*. Here we can reasonably hope to establish what the authors of the document took the myth to explain and what they hoped to accomplish by using it in the way they did. The myth in terms of which they devised their account was certainly not of their own making. It was made, like the English language itself, by the accumulated efforts of the community to which they belonged. But, requiring, as they did, an argument to support their demands, they turned to the common stock of collective representations and took from it whatever would best suit their purpose.

We must, therefore, take with a grain of salt the suggestion that myths can be read as statements by a society about itself. In the social intercourse of men myths occur only as arguments; and an argument is invariably a specific response to a particular state of affairs. To proffer a myth is to perform a deliberate act, and an individual stamp will be left upon it no matter how orthodox the narrator tries to be. It is true that a particular mythical account must be couched in terms of collective representations. But it cannot itself be a collective representation.

However, if the content and meaning of a myth is not determined by the society in which it circulates, what about its purpose? In telling a myth, the myth-maker not only intends his audience to understand the message he has in mind; he also intends to make them behave in a certain way. He performs a practical act which, like all practical acts, has intended consequences or purposes. Can we regard these purposes as being, in some sense or another, socially determined? Malinowski and his followers argue that we can.

Myth, Malinowski asserts, has a social function, and it is in terms of its social function that it must be defined. 'The function of myth,' he tells us, 'is to strengthen tradition and endow it with a greater value and prestige by tracing it back to a higher, better, more supernatural reality of initial events.' More particularly, myth 'expresses, enhances, and codifies belief; it safeguards and enforces morality; it vouches for the efficiency of ritual and contains practical rules for the guidance of man'.[33] It may, in some cases relieve 'sociological strain' by covering up an inconsistency introduced into a society in the course of migration or economic change; it might help reconcile men to certain permanent features of the human condition, such as death; or it may serve to glorify a certain social group or to justify an anomalous status. And the functionalist student of politics might add that the function of political myths is to legitimize the authority of governments and to improve the solidarity of political groups.

Malinowski defines the term 'function' as 'the satisfaction of a need'.[24] The activity of eating, for example, has as its function the satisfaction of hunger. The satisfaction of hunger is a state of affairs brought about by the activity of eating. It is a consequence of that activity. And, generally, when Malinowski speaks of the functions of activities, he means their consequences. An activity may, of course, have more than one consequence, and some of these consequences may not be those directly intended. 'A group of primitives,' Geertz observes, 'sets out, in all honesty, to pray for rain and ends by strengthening its social solidarity; a ward politician sets out to get or remain near the trough and ends by mediating between unassimilated immigrant groups and an impersonal governmental bureaucracy; an ideologist sets out to air his grievances and finds himself contributing, through the diversionary power of his illusions, to the continued viability of the very system that grieves him.'[25] It is clear that we can explain an activity by reference to its consequences if the consequences meant are *intended*, that is, if they are the conscious purposes of the activity. But it is a different matter when the consequences in question are *unintended*. Stepping onto busy streets may, with a certain statistical regularity, result in the unintended consequence of being knocked down by a bus; but it is difficult to see how this can help explain the activity of stepping onto busy streets. None the less, when Malinowski speaks of the functions of an activity, he includes both its intended and its unintended consequences; and he insists that an activity can be *explained* in terms of its function. This suggests that he regards the function of an activity as being in some sense its purpose, even though it may consist of unintended consequences.

On the face of it, Malinowski's approach seems perfectly sound. Biologists, for instance, legitimately employ functional or teleological language in their explanations. Such explanations usually take the form of asserting that, within a specified system, it is the function or purpose of a particular organ to maintain a certain characteristic state or activity of that system. It might, for example, be argued that it is a function of the kidney to eliminate waste products thus maintaining that chemical composition of the blood without which the organism as a whole would cease to exist. As Nagel has pointed out, arguments of this kind in no way imply the operation of conscious purposes or ends-in-view. Nothing is asserted except that the activity of a given organ has specified and regular consequences for the whole system of which it is a constituent part. A functional statement can, without loss of meaning, be translated into a simple statement of cause and effect. Instead of saying that y is a function of x, we can say that x causes y. The sole difference is one of selective attention. While a functional statement connotes that the activity under examination takes place in a directively organized system, its non-functional equivalent does not.[26]

The most common interpretation of Malinowski's view is that he thinks of a culture as being a system in all relevant respects similar to an organism. Men, he observes, are subject to various needs which they must satisfy by acting upon the environment in which they find themselves. They must feed, house, clothe and protect themselves; and, in order to do so, they must create artefacts, invent techniques, form co-operative groups, and much else besides. So it is that, in order to satisfy their 'primary' or 'basic' needs, men create that artificial environment which Malinowski calls culture. However, the satisfaction of basic or primary needs breeds what Malinowski terms 'secondary' or 'derived' needs. Many of these secondary needs can be classed under the heading of the need to maintain in proper working order the artefacts, activities and institutions devised to satisfy the primary needs. Political institutions, and codes of moral behaviour are, in Malinowski's view, created for this purpose, and so are myths.[27] There is no doubt that Malinowski thinks of myths, morals and the like as functioning to prevent rather than promote structural change. But it is no part of his thesis that a properly functioning culture is incapable of change or innovation. All his theory implies is that, at any given moment, a culture is a self-sustaining system in which 'every custom, material object, idea and belief fulfils some vital function, has some task to accomplish, represents an indispensible part within a working whole'.[28] In other words, although a culture may constantly change, it never loses its organic coherence. It is always an 'instrumental apparatus' which displays the life and unity of a living organism.

So Malinowski argues that every activity is functional in the senes that it satisfies a need and that this is the reason why it is performed. However, an activity may, in Malinowski's view, have a function of which the actor himself is unaware. This is especially the case where the satisfaction of secondary needs is concerned, for such needs are, properly speaking, needs of the system as a whole rather than the felt needs of any one individual, and it is here that Malinowski's theory meets with its most serious difficulties.

Asked how we identify the need by which an activity is determined, Malinowski replies that we do so by observing what, in fact, that activity achieves. If, for example, we observe that, in a certain culture, myth-making enhances social solidarity, we can conclude that members of that culture have a need for social solidarity and that this is why they make myths. Unfortunately, this explains nothing; for if we broaden the scope of our observation, we will find that other activities, such as church-going, also enhance social solidarity, and it is clear that, if the need for social solidarity can be satisfied in more ways than one, then myth-making cannot be explained in terms of this need alone. We may even find that, in some societies, myth-making serves to disrupt social solidarity by (for instance) accentuating class differences; and this would compel us either to draw the unhelpful conclusion that myth-making has many functions some of which are mutually contradictory, or to assert that the societies in question have no need to enhance social solidarity.

The source of these difficulties is, of course, the fact that cultures are not, in any significant respect, comparable with the members of a biological species. The members of a biological species are very much like one another, and the biologist can easily define the class of systems he is talking about, specify the parts of these systems and enumerate their characteristic states or activities. Cultures, on the other hand, are notoriously diverse. The activities and institutions found in one are rarely the same as those found in another. Each culture is unique. It may be that the same 'vital functions' are performed in them all, but they are often performed in different ways. And this makes it impossible for the social scientist to generalize about activities and their functions. He cannot assume that, because a certain activity performs a certain function in one culture, it will perform the same function in another. Nor can he assume that, because all cultures have similar functions to be performed, they will contain similar activities and institutions. In short, he cannot systematically link the supposed needs of a society with the specific activities performed within it. And, even if he could, the crucial defect of his position would still remain. For, to assert that a particular activity has certain particular consequences does not, in any way, explain that activity. Nothing, for example, is explained about the activity of the kidney by showing that it results in the elimination of waste products from the blood. To be explained, the activity of the kidney would itself have to be shown to be the consequence of other activities. Effects can be explained in terms of their causes, but causes cannot be explained in terms of their effects. The only circumstance in which the effects of an activity have any explanatory power is when they can be shown to be the intended consequences or conscious purposes of the activity.[29]

It is certainly true that the propagation of myths may have far-reaching consequences not intended by the myth-maker; and if our main concern is with the society in which such myths occur, then these unintended consequences must be traced and somehow accounted for. But, if we wish to explain the myths themselves, we must concentrate instead on the conscious purposes of the myth-maker. There is a further point. As Leach remarks, it is a clear implication of Malinowski's theory 'that the myths of any one culture should be mutually consistent'. In point of fact, they rarely are. Among the Kachins of Highland Burma, Leach found that myths are used to support conflicting claims or to defend vested interests against attack, and that, so far from being mutually consistent, the myths of the Kachin flatly contradict one another. 'Myth and ritual,' says Leach, 'is a language of signs in terms of which claims to rights and status are expressed, but it is a language of argument, not a chorus of harmony.'[30] And the same holds, as we shall see, for the political myths of Western European societies.

Let us now return to Cassirer's suggestion that, in mythical thought, 'we do not meet with individual confessions'. Malinowski has certainly done us a service in stressing the practical and social character of myth-making, but we cannot agree that myths are in any strict sense social products. Societies are not organisms which can act apart from the individual members of which they are composed. Furthermore, though most mythical accounts are versions of established myths and therefore appear to be nothing more than reiterations of traditional lore, the appearance is, as I have argued, deceptive. A mythical utterance is always to some degree an individual confession; and a myth, considered apart from the individual utterances in which it is expressed, is a non-existent entity, an object fit only for metaphysical speculation. Besides, we must not suppose that mythical thinking allows no scope whatsoever for the determined innovator. It sometimes happens that an individual myth-maker selects elements from a variety of existing myths and other kinds of doctrine and fits them together to make a mythical account which is not simply a version of any single known myth. Lévi-Strauss has drawn attention to this process and calls it 'bricolage'. Just as the handyman or 'bricoleur' improvises a new artefact from the odds and ends he finds lying about in his workshop, so the myth-maker 'builds up structured sets, not directly with other structured sets, but by using the remains and debris of events . . . fossilized evidence of the history of an individual or a society'.[31] Lévi-Strauss is no doubt right in supposing that many myths are made in this fashion. Indeed, Cassirer, in contradiction to his own thesis, describes the political myths of modern times as 'artificial things fabricated by very skilful and cunning artisans'.[32] Plato's myths do, of course, fall short of being genuine mythical accounts. But this is not because they were deliberate fictions. It is because they were not seriously meant to be believed.

The structuralist theory of myth

We must now consider the structuralist theory of myth, a theory which has, in recent years, become fashionable and which is largely associated with the work of Lévi-Strauss. Many proponents of the theory (Sebag, Althusser, Barthes) present it as an extension of Marxism; but all would agree that, as a method of analysis, it owes its immediate inspiration to Ferdinand de Saussure and the Prague school of linguistics.

Political Myth/53

In his *Course in General Linguistics*, Saussure emphasized two main points concerning the study of language. Firstly, he drew attention to the distinction between *langue*, defined as 'the whole set of linguistic habits which allow an individual to understand and be understood', and *parole*, by which he meant the various utterances or acts of expression made in the language. It is, he insisted, *langue* and not *parole* which is the proper object of linguistic analysis.[33] Secondly, he pointed out that a language can be studied either as it evolves over time (diachronically) or in abstraction from its existence in time (synchronically); and it was the latter course that he recommended.[34]

In addition to these two broad points, Saussure laid down a number of principles, the first and most important of which was that a language is 'a system of arbitrary signs'. By this, he did not mean that the individual can associate concepts and sounds to form words as his fancy strikes him. (The association of particular sounds with particular concepts is, in fact, established by the linguistic community to which the individual belongs.) He meant that there is no necessary or natural relationship between the concept and the sound which serves as its signifier. As he put it: 'The idea of "sister" is not linked by any inner relationship to the succession of sounds s-ö-r which serves as its signifier in French: that it could be represented equally by just any other sequence is proved by the differences among languages and by the very existence of different languages.'[35]

Because of the arbitrary nature of the linguistic sign a language is, according to Saussure, 'a system of pure values'. His point was this. Thought, considered apart from its expression in words, is nothing but a shapeless and indistinct mass. This indistinct mass becomes a system of distinct concepts only in so far as segments of thought are associated with segments of sound. The reverse also holds true. Sound is not, of itself, divided into distinct entities. It becomes so divided only through segments of it being associated with specific concepts. 'Each linguistic term is a member, an *articulus* in which an idea is fixed in a sound and a sound becomes the sign of an idea.'[36] In other words, the materials of which a language is made have no 'positive value' of their own. Taken by themselves, sounds are distinct only in the negative sense that they are different from other sounds, and the same is true for thoughts. 'But,' Saussure remarks, 'the statement that everything in language is negative is true only if the signified and the signifier are considered separately; when we consider the sign in its totality, we have something that is positive in its own class. A linguistic system is a series of differences of sound combined with a series of differences of ideas; but the pairing of a certain number of acoustical signs with as many cuts made from the mass of thought engenders a system of values; and this system serves as the effective link between the phonic and psychological elements within each sign.'[37]

Guided by these suggestions, Roman Jakobsen and his colleagues set out to explore the character of language as a synchronic system composed of basic speech-sounds or phonemes. Briefly, they discovered that we discriminate between basic speech-sounds in terms of binary oppositions: nasal/oral, grave/acute, sharp/flat etc. Each term of such an opposition they called a 'distinctive feature', and a phoneme, they suggested, is a bundle made up of several such distinctive features. Thus, the Turkish sound 'u' is found to be a diffuse, grave and flat sound; and it is thanks to the fact that each of these three distinctive features has an opposite that we are able to distinguish 'u' from the other phonemes that occur in the Turkish language.[38] Furthermore, Jakobsen argued, distinctive features are combined to make phonemes and phonemes are combined to make morphemes and words according to regular laws which can be determined by empirical investigation. Language, in short, has a structure which the mind, with its innate tendency to make binary oppositions, creates; and so it is that what would otherwise be a continuum of undifferentiated noise is reduced to a phonic system capable of conveying meaning.

The achievement of the structural linguists will, Lévi-Strauss declares, 'play the same renovating role with respect to the social sciences that nuclear physics, for example, has played for the physical sciences'.[39] Hitherto, he observes, the main obstacle to the introduction of scientific methods into the study of human behaviour has been the fact that men act according to rules which, to a large extent, they make themselves and can therefore change or break at will. Furthermore, the social scientist often cannot but modify the very activities he is studying and thus prejudice the results of his investigation. (Anthropologists in the field do not study primitive communities. They study primitive communities responding to the presence of an anthropologist.) But language, according to the structural linguists, is governed by laws which, because they are imposed by the unconscious activity of the mind, cannot be interfered with either by the observer or by the speakers themselves. And, if this holds for language, might it not also hold for other social institutions? May we not surmise that all forms of social life 'consist of systems of behaviour that represent the projection, on the level of conscious and socialized thought, of universal laws which regulate the unconscious activities of the mind?'[40] Lévi-Strauss's answer is that we may. Underlying every institution and activity (he suggests) there is an unconscious structure which governs the activity of the mind and thus stands in a causal relationship to the various social phenomena which anthropologists have puzzled over for so long and to so little effect.

This view has much to recommend it. Not only does it promise to introduce scientific methods where such methods are conspicuously absent; it also enables us to theorize at a high level of abstraction. We can, at the structural level, compare and relate the whole range of economic, social and cultural activities in any given society, for they are all, at bottom, manifestations of the same reality. It is important to note that, for Lévi-Strauss, a structure is not a conceptual scheme or model which the social scientist creates by generalizing from a number of observed cases and which, ultimately, exists nowhere but in his own mind. It is itself a part of reality. It is the actual unconscious process which gives all social activities their appearance of order. In the social sciences, therefore, 'it is not comparison that supports generalization, but the other way around . . . it is necessary and sufficient to grasp the unconscious structure underlying each institution and each custom, in order to obtain a principle of interpretation valid for other institutions and other customs, provided of course that the analysis is carried far enough.'[41]

Furthermore, the theory has, for Lévi-Strauss, the advantage that it helps overcome the opposition between the collective nature of culture and its manifestations in the individual, since, in the last analysis, the so-called collective consciousness is 'no more than the expression, on the level of individual thought and behaviour, of certain time and space modalities of the universal laws which make up the unconscious activity of the mind'.[42] The defect of the theory is, of course, that the structures of which Lévi-Strauss speaks cannot be observed empirically. They are not phenomena; they are what lie behind phenomena. How do we know that they are, in fact, there? But, leaving this aside, let us see how Lévi-Strauss applies his views to the study of myths.

The academic study of myths, Lévi-Strauss contends, finds itself in the same predicament as pre-scientific linguistics; for, in academic mythology, the assumption still prevails that where similar symbols and motifs occur they must have similar meanings, just as linguists before Saussure had assumed that there must be a natural connection between sounds and the ideas these sounds signified. As in linguistics, so in mythology; we must look, not to the manifest content, but to the way this content is structured. 'If there is a meaning to be found in mythology, it cannot reside in the isolated elements which enter into the composition of a myth, but only in the way those elements are combined.'[43]

To identify the 'elements' of a myth, we must, Lévi-Strauss tells us, break down the story into the shortest possible sentences: 'Cadmus kills the dragon', 'Oedipus marries his mother' and so forth. When this is done, it will be apparent that the similarities between various of the elements thus isolated make it possible to sort them into separate 'bundles'. For example, the elements, 'Cadmus kills the dragon' and 'Oedipus kills the Sphinx' belong in the same 'bundle' because they both deal with the slaying of monsters; and, since monsters are chthonian beings, this 'bundle' of elements signifies 'the denial of the autochthonous origin of man'. It is, according to Lévi-Strauss, such 'bundles' of similar elements which are the 'true constituent units' of a myth.[44]

He now goes on to suggest that these units invariably come in pairs of opposites. If, in the Oedipus myth, we have one unit denying the autochthonous origin of man, we will, without fail, find another which affirms the autochthonous origin of man. We can, therefore, group these units into pairs of binary oppositions, such as, life/death, male/female, patrilocal residence/matrilocal residence, raw/cooked, etc. Furthermore, these various pairs of opposites can be collected into several 'conceptual schemes' according to whether they deal with (for instance) cosmological, sociological or economic matters. And these conceptual schemes and their relationship with one another can be expressed in a diagram or a series of diagrams which, we are told, will represent the global structure of the myth analysed.[45]

Now, what will the structure of a myth tell us? It will, Lévi-Strauss asserts, make plain the meaning of a myth. Thus, in his deliberately simplified version of the Oedipus myth, Lévi-Strauss isolates four constituent units which make up two sets of binary oppositions: 'denial of the autochthonous origin of man/affirmation of the autochthonous origin of man' and 'underrating blood-relations/overrating blood-relations'. The myth as a whole, he suggests, is an attempt to reconcile the belief that men originally sprang from the earth with the knowledge that men are, in fact, born of their parents. Of course, the two views are logically incompatible. But the myth mediates between them by suggesting that they are related in a way comparable to the relationship between overrating blood-relations and underrating blood-relations. That is, although the two beliefs are diametrically opposed, they can coexist with one another because they are both within the realm of practical possibilities. In this way, the paradox is overcome; or, at least, it is obscured and thus laid to rest. And this is the general purpose of myths: 'to provide a logical model capable of overcoming a contradiction'. In other words, myth is the method men adopt to make coherent and therefore acceptable whatever is fundamentally self-contradictory in their beliefs or in their practical life. And it works by associating the original contradiction with a series of progressively less extreme contradictions. Thus mythical thought, Lévi-Strauss tells us, 'always progresses from the awareness of oppositions toward their resolution'.[46]

In this fashion, the myth-maker conveys a message to his audience. But the message is one of which neither he nor his audience are aware. Indeed, Lévi-Strauss insists that structural analysis tells us nothing about how or what men think. 'We do not,' he says, 'pretend to show how men think in their myths, but how myths think themselves in men, and without their awareness.'[47] This leads him to another point about the interpretation of myths. Since myths operate below the level of consciousness, a myth has to be repeated often and in many different forms if its meaning is to be conveyed. For this reason, there are usually many versions of the same myth in circulation; and we also find apparently different myths which structural analysis reveals to be, in fact, variants of the same theme. So far as Lévi-Strauss is concerned, there is no such thing as the true version of a myth. All versions and variants convey the same meaning, and all do it equally well or badly. The objective, he tells us, is to collect, analyse and (at the structural level) compare all available versions and, by thus treating them as a single communication, to extract the hidden doctrine which they contain.[48]

Such, then, is the method Lévi-Strauss recommends, and it is not difficult to see why it has met with so much sceptical comment. First of all, his claim that myth is a special language looks very much like an analogy, and, like any analogy, it is suspect. We do indeed speak of the language of myth, just as we speak of the language of morals, the language of science and even the language of love. But we do not mean that these are languages in the sense that French, German and Latin are languages. What we mean is that they are specialized codes, each of which employs concepts and rules peculiarly its own. These codes may, metaphorically, be described as 'languages', but they differ from languages in the ordinary sense of the term. In making, for instance, a scientific statement, we must, of course, use scientific terms and adhere to the canons of scientific reasoning, but this is not sufficient. We must, in addition, have recourse to one of the common languages such as French, German or Latin. Otherwise we would not be able to express ourselves at all. And the same goes for mythical statements. Myth may well be, like science, a code. But this does not make it a language. We cannot make a mythical statement using no 'language' other than that of myth. To convey anything at all, a myth must find expression in a verbal utterance made in one of the common languages which the myth-maker has at his command.

It will not help us much to describe myth as a 'meta-language', for, whichever way we slice it, the fact remains that language is a system of pure values whereas myth is not. The elements or basic speech-sounds of a language are, we recall, devoid of any positive value or meaning. The same cannot be said for the elements of which a myth is composed. These elements are, in fact, full-blown statements, and it would be eccentric to suggest that such statements are in themselves meaningless. The statement 'Oedipus kills the Sphinx' does not lose all meaning when we consider it in isolation from its context. It retains its literal meaning; and it has, to this extent, a positive value of its own. Furthermore, the structural linguists had maintained that a linguistic sign is composed of a sequence of sounds (the signifier) and a concept (the signified), and that there is no natural or necessary connection between the two. In myth, we also have constituent units composed of a signifier and a signified. However, the signifier is not a sequence of sounds but a bundle of statements while the signified, to which these statements are linked, is a general idea or proposition; and the connection between them is anything but arbitrary. The question as to whether the episodes of Cadmus and Oedipus have anything to do with the autochthonous origin of man *can*, in fact, be discussed and reasons *can* be given for supposing that there is (or is not) a connection. And, in this respect, the constituent units of a myth differ radically from the constituent units of language. In myths, to put it differently, we are dealing not with signs but with symbols. And, as Saussure remarked: 'One characteristic of the symbol is that it is never wholly arbitrary; it is not empty, for there is the rudiment of a natural bond between the signifier and the signified. The symbol of justice, a pair of scales, could not be replaced by just any other symbol, such as a chariot '[49]

These differences between myth and language are, I think, crucial. They are certainly far-reaching enough to throw doubt on the suggestion that we can apply to myths the analytical techniques which the structural linguists developed in the study of language. In any case, the view that the meaning of a myth is to be found, not in its contents, but in the way these contents are structured is based on a misconception of what structural analysis can do. No structural linguist has ever claimed that it is possible, by structural analysis alone, to establish the *meaning* of any particular utterance. To make such a claim would be to reassert the exploded hypothesis that there is a natural connection between sounds and their meaning. All structural analysis can do is help us understand how it is possible for a word or statement to have any meaning at all. It uncovers the system or code which allows meanings to be conveyed, but it does not tell us what those meanings are.[50]

In effect, Lévi-Strauss's analysis suffers from the same confusion we noticed in connection with the Idealist theory of myth. No myth is a mere jumble of statements which have to be put into order like the pieces of a jig-saw puzzle before they make sense. A myth is a narrative of events in dramatic form, and, as such, it has a manifest meaning. Lévi-Strauss does not deny this; but he argues that the manifest meaning of a myth is not its true meaning. Although the myth-maker and his audience may think they understand their myth, they are wrong, for the myth is, in fact, a coded statement conveying a hidden meaning. And, in order to elicit this hidden meaning, we must reduce the myth to its elements, re-organize them into bundles and examine the way these bundles are related. But clearly, in doing this, we do not discover the *meaning* of the myth. We discover the attitudes and concepts which the myth presupposes. The conceptual structures of which Levi-Strauss speaks merely prescribe the subjective limits within which an act of communication takes place. They give us its form, but they cannot give us its meaning. The only meaning a statement can have is the one it is understood to have by those who conduct the conversation in which it occurs.

It remains only to add that, in adopting an essentially Idealist point of view, Lévi-Strauss abandons himself to an approach as arbitrary as that of the classical allegorists. He tells us to isolate the elements of a myth by breaking the story down into the shortest possible sentences. But he does not add that we must thereby eliminate those features of the story which we regard as irrelevant and that we can do this only if we have already decided what the myth is about. Similarly, the business of allocating the elements of a myth to various bundles each signifying a specific idea presupposes a prior knowledge of what ideas are at work in the myth. How, for instance, do we know that the elements 'Cadmus kills the dragon' and 'Oedipus kills the Sphinx' both signify the denial of the autochthonous origin of man? For the ancient Greeks, they might have signified something else altogether. Indeed, there are so many differences between the two episodes that we could easily argue that they belong in quite different bundles. The dragon is killed, the Sphinx commits suicide; Cadmus acts out of vengeance, Odeipus acts in self-defence; the dragon lives near a spring, the Sphinx lives on top of a rock, and so forth. There are, in short, many possible bundles to which these elements might be allocated according to the tastes and predispositions of the interpreter.

It is, therefore, not surprising that Lévi-Strauss is able to discover all kinds of hidden meanings in the myths he analyses. He has put them there himself. If we treat a myth, not as a statement possessing a coherence of its own, but as a collection of materials to be rewritten and reorganized in whatever way we please, there is no end to the meanings we can discover; nor is there any criterion by which we can judge one interpretation to be more satisfactory than another.

Myths as the expression of timeless truths

In his *Phenomenology of Mind*, Hegel remarked that, behind the curtain of appearances, 'there is nothing to be seen unless we ourselves go behind there, as much in order that we may thereby see, as that there may be something behind there which can be seen'.[51] Hegel, at least, knew what he was about. His intellectual heirs, however, persist in forgetting that the reality they detect behind appearances is nothing but their own reflection; and nowhere is this more evident than in the study of myths. We have discussed some of the more sober victims of this peculiarly academic disease, but there are many others whose views are so general as to defy analysis. Schniewind tells us that myth is 'the expression of unobservable realities in terms of observable phenomena'; Jaspers argues that 'the language of myth' is 'the language of a reality that is not empirical, but existential'; and Guenon insists that myths refer to realities 'which, by their very nature, are inexpressible, at least directly and in ordinary language'.[52] In every myth, we are assured, there is a profound mystery, an implicit reference to some transcendental realm of timeless truths which only the learned can hope to penetrate. There is, of course, little to be said about this approach, except that the interpretations it offers are often more obscure than the myths they are supposed to elucidate. Some theorists, however, take a less subjective stand. While maintaining that myths are indeed concerned with a realm of timeless truths, they argue that the reference to this realm is, in any true myth, not darkly hinted at but made unmistakably explicit.

This is, for instance, the position of Mircea Eliade. A genuine myth, he tells us, can be identified by the presence of two distinguishing marks. It is, firstly, a story which relates an event that took place in primordial time, 'the fabled time of the beginnings', and, secondly, it invariably deals with the origins of things. It is the story of how something was created, 'how, through the deeds of Supernatural Beings, a reality came into existence, be it the whole of reality, the Cosmos, or only a particular kind of human behavior, an institution'. In myth, then, a thing is explained when it is referred back to a unique primordial event. This event does not itself require explanation. It is simply stated as a fact, and the myth-maker's audience is expected to take it on trust. They can do so partly because the normal criteria for plausibility do not apply to the strange and sacred world of primordial time and partly because a myth does, after all, deal with what is obviously real. 'The cosmogonic myth is "true" because the existence of the world is there to prove it; the myth of the origin of death is equally true because man's mortality proves it, and so on.' In short, the very facts a myth is supposed to explain are taken as evidence for the truth of the myth.[53]

In Eliade's view, what happens in the mythical world of primordial time is of practical significance in that it is taken to be exemplary. It becomes the paradigm for how things should be done ever after. The main reason for this is the belief (supposedly inseparable from mythical thought) that all things are endowed with life and that the source of all life, strength and efficacy is the supernatural force at work in the beginnings. It is, according to Eliade, a corollary of this belief that, as things recede in time from their origin, they lose their strength, decay and eventually die. The only way to restore things to the bloom of their youth is, therefore, to repeat the act which brought them into being in the first place. Ritual and myth are, Eliade suggests, such attempts to recover the perfection of the beginnings, to restore to things the vital force at work when the world was new; and the constant preoccupation of the myth-maker is to return *ad fontes*, to the origins. Mythical time is, in short, reversible. What was once done is not forever lost; it may in the fulness of time repeat itself. Whether explicitly or implicitly, every myth is, therefore, a story of death and rebirth, of an end or *eschatos* which is simultaneously a new beginning.[54]

Evidently, there is much in Eliade's view that coincides with our own. He insists that a myth is always a story believed to be true and that it serves as an explanation for some aspect of men's present experience. He further argues that myths are practical arguments, at least in the special sense that they present past events as precedents or paradigms for present action—a point to which we shall have to return. But the difficulty is that, if we confine the term 'myth' to stories of the supernatural events that took place in primordial time, then no event known to have occurred in historical time can be made the subject of a mythical account. This would exclude from being myths nearly all the doctrines with which the present study is concerned. It is true that many political myths embody the theme of loss and recovery, death and rebirth, or whatever one wishes to call it. But the theme is not always treated in the way Eliade's thesis requires. For example, in many revolutionary myths, the new beginning which follows the *eschatos* is not in fact presented as a return to the origins.

In any case, Eliade makes it clear that the theme of eternal return is not in itself sufficient to make a story a myth. To be a myth, a story must assert the abiding presence of primordial and sacred realities in the temporal world of everyday affairs. And this is something most political myths fail to do. Even the Roman Foundation Myth, which otherwise conforms closely to Eliade's definition, falls short in this one important respect. It is not that the Romans lacked any notion of primordial time. We find it expressed in their legend of the golden age, the peaceful and prosperous reign of Saturn. But this only makes it all the more striking that they did not regard the foundation of their city as having taken place in this 'fabled time of the beginnings'. So far as the Romans were concerned, the act of foundation was a matter of historical record. There was some dispute as to the date. Cato placed the founding of the city in 755 BC whereas Varro's more careful calculation made it 753 BC. But the point remains that the city was founded, not in the sacred world of primordial time, but in the profane world of everyday affairs. Similarly, the Levellers and Diggers of seventeenth-century England made a clear distinction between the historical Anglo-Saxon constitution and the primordial Garden of Eden; and it was in the former that they found their most pertinent mythical precedents.

There is nothing wrong with regarding as myths only those stories which relate the creative deeds performed by the gods in primordial time. Ultimately, myths are what the mythologist defines them to be. But Eliade's definition is unnecessarily arbitrary; and it is arbitrary because it defines myths in terms of their subject-matter. Some myths do, of course, tell us about the intervention of supernatural powers in an otherwise natural world; but many myths confine themselves to the deeds of men. And, in political myths, the supernatural tends to play a very small role, if indeed it plays any role at all. This is not to say that the supernatural has no place whatsoever in a political myth. The institutions of a political society are often sanctified by being given a divine origin. But political myths can more easily dispense with the supernatural than can, say, nature-myths. And the reason for this is clear. If a myth is to explain things by telling the story of how they come about, it must be a narrative of things done, of acts or deeds; it must have *dramatis personae*, for, if it did not, it would lack dramatic form. It is, of course, implausible to explain natural phenomena as being the products of merely human activity, and that, in part, is why nature-myths resort to supernatural agents. But political institutions and events are a different case. Here there is nothing implausible about supposing that human agencies are at work, and a political myth can, accordingly, make do without having recourse to gods or demons.

T. H. Gaster's view of myth is more general than that of Eliade and thus avoids some of the difficulties I have mentioned. According to Gaster, myth is simply 'any presentation of the actual in terms of the ideal'. This characteristic, he says, is particularly apparent in the relationship between myth and ritual; for, while a ritual presents a situation as an event in which actual living individuals are involved, a myth presents the same situation 'as something transpiring (rather than occurring) concurrently in eternity and as involving preterpunctual, indesinent beings of whom living men and women are but the temporal incarnations'.[55] But it is not only in connection with rituals that myths occur. In early doctrines of divine kingship, for instance, the king in his human aspect epitomizes the character of a community as it exists at a particular moment in time, and, in his divine aspect, he represents the same community conceived as an ideal or transcendental entity. Similarly a holy city or building is one that has an ideal or heavenly equivalent, and wars are often considered as conflicts between nations in their ideal and timeless aspect. In myth, then, we have a world which, though radically different from the one in which we live, runs parallel to it in the sense that there are things in the one which have their counterparts in the other. These worlds are distinguished as the actual from the ideal or the temporal from the eternal. And anything can, in principle, be 'mythologized' by being allotted a heavenly or ideal doppelgänger.

It is, I think, fair to say that, according to Gaster, myth occurs whenever men ascribe a real existence to their symbolic abstractions. As Gaster himself seems partly aware, this notion includes much that we would not normally regard as myth. Indeed, the term as he employs it can be made to cover almost any expression of vulgar Idealism. Gaster is, no less than Eliade, entitled to his own definition of myth. But, in an enquiry of the kind we have launched, so broad a use of the term can only cause confusion, and must therefore be rejected.

However, his view that myths always present the immediately particular as being something timelessly ideal is not so easily disposed of. It is true that a certain timeless quality is to be found in most mythical accounts, and especially in political myths. In fact, wherever an episode from the past (such as the founding of Rome or the storming of the Bastille) is put forward as an example to guide men's present activity, it inevitably loses its 'historical' character and becomes, as Gaster would say, an ideal. But in this there is, on reflection, nothing mysterious. When a past episode is treated as a paradigm for the present state of affairs, it is no longer important to think of it as having occurred at a particular point in time. It ceases to be a 'historical' fact. But it is not thereby transposed into primordial time, as Eliade would have it; nor does it necessarily find a home in Gaster's heavenly realm of transcendental entities. It becomes quite simply a precedent which is timeless or eternal only in the trivial sense that the practical purpose for which it is being used does not require an insistence on its historicity.[56] And we might add that, although this phenomenon frequently occurs in mythical arguments, it occurs in other kinds of argument as well and is, therefore, not to be regarded as a definitive feature of myth.

Chapter Three

The genesis of the Roman Foundation Myth

Many political myths are what we may call foundation myths. They tell the tale of how a political society came to be founded. Although such myths are common enough in our own time (particularly in states established during a revolutionary upheaval or a war of national liberation) it is in the political literature of classical antiquity that the best examples are to be found. Most of these classical foundation myths were of strictly local significance and survive only as perfunctory notices in the compilations of Strabo and Pausanias. But there were some which, for one reason or another, attracted a sufficiently general interest to find a place in the common culture of the ancient world; and, of these, the Roman Foundation Myth is by far the most famous and the most fully documented.

The earliest extant version of the myth is to be found in the fragments surviving from the *Histories* of Fabius Pictor and Naevius's *Punica*, both of which date from the closing years of the Second Punic War (218–201 BC). There are further and more elaborate references to the myth in the literary remains of the following century when Rome was establishing her hegemony in the Mediterranean basin. (Ennius's *Annales* and Cato's *Origines* are here of particular importance.) Then, at the time of Cicero and the collapse of the old republic, the myth undergoes extensive revision, only to be restored to something like its earlier form under the auspices of the Caesars. Virgil's *Aeneid* and Livy's *Ab urbe condita* belong to this period and are each, in their own way, imbued with the outlook of the new order Augustus established.

The tale, as we have it in Fabius and Naevius,[1] tells the story of how Aeneas, with a band of Trojan refugees, escapes from the sack of Troy and, after a perilous voyage, effects a landing on the coast of Latium. Here the Trojans establish themselves, and the descendants of Aeneas become kings of Alba Longa. Several generations later, the succession devolves upon two brothers, Numitor and Amulius. Amulius manages to usurp the throne for himself, but, fearing that Numitor's daughter Ilia might bear children, he makes her a vestal virgin. However, his ruse fails, for she soon proves to be pregnant and, protesting that she was seduced by Mars, gives birth to twin sons, Romulus and Remus. Undismayed, Amulius sets the twins adrift in a trough, but the Tiber deposits them unharmed at the foot of the Palatine where they are first suckled by a she-wolf and later reared by local shepherds. In due course, the twins return to Alba Longa and, having restored Numitor to his rightful place, they lead a band of colonists back to the future site of Rome. Here they take auspices to determine which of them shall found the projected city. The auspices favour Romulus; but the foundation is marred by tragedy, for, while Romulus is building the city walls, he quarrels with his brother and kills him, thus becoming the sole founder and first king of the city.

It is clear that the account which Naevius and Fabius gave of Rome's origin was a version of an already established tradition. It is equally clear that it is an amalgam of two quite distinct stories, that of Aeneas and that of Romulus and Remus. The former asserts that Rome was founded by immigrants from Asia Minor, and the latter points to a Latin origin for the Roman people. Although the story of Romulus is probably the older of the two,[2] the earliest Greek accounts ignore the legend altogether and ascribe the founding of the city to a Rhome or a Rhomos. It is not until the fourth century, when the Greeks had learned more about the native traditions of Rome, that we get something approaching the story as we know it. Alcimus, for example, tells us that Aeneas had a son, Romulus, whose daughter Alba, gave birth to Rhomos, the founder of Rome; and Callias asserts that a Trojan woman, Rhome, married king Latinus and that their sons, Rhomos and Rhomylus, founded the city named after their mother.[3] It is difficult to know what to make of such accounts, but the story of the twin brothers, Romulus and Remus looks a bit like a compromise between native Roman traditions and Greek historical speculation. Certainly, it received only a grudging acceptance among the Romans themselves. In all Roman accounts, Remus or Rhomos appears as something of an interloper; he plays a relatively minor role in the story, and many of the later historians do not mention him at all.[4]

The circumstances in which the Aeneas legend became established are equally obscure. The story is almost certainly of Greek origin. Aeneas appears briefly in the *Iliad*, and Hellinicus of Lesbos (fifth century) described the flight of Aeneas from Troy to Aenea in Chalcidice.[5] Though none of the early Greek historians mention Aeneas's voyage to Italy, there is archaeological evidence to suggest that Aeneas was celebrated as founder-hero in many cities of Southern Etruria and that the Etruscans brought Aeneas to Rome when, in the sixth century, they extended their rule to the plain of Latium.[6] If, as many historians insist, Aeneas was known in Etruscan Rome, chances are that he was known as the symbol of foreign domination. Indeed, Galinsky has suggested that, with the expulsion of the Etruscans and the Roman counter-attack against the cities of Southern Etruria, the story of Rome's Trojan origins was suppressed. There is, in fact, no evidence for the survival of the Aeneas legend in the early republican period of Rome. Instead, the Romans show a marked tendency to adopt Greek traditions in cult, art and law. In 484 BC, for example, the patricians introduced from Lavinium the Greek cult of the Dioscuri, and, in the same year Rome began her wars with the Etruscan city of Veii. A passage in Livy, which may well reflect an ancient tradition, compares the siege of Veii with the siege of Troy; but it is the Romans who are cast in the role of the Greeks and their Etruscan enemies are presented as Trojans.[7] Etruscan influence no doubt survived in Rome (particularly among patrician families of Etruscan descent), and the tradition of Rome's Trojan origins was not entirely forgotten. But, as Galinsky remarks, 'so long as the Etruscans remained Rome's formidable opponents in Italy, the Romans were not inclined to associate the Etruscan Aeneas with the foundation of their own city'.[8] In short, the signs are that, during the first two centuries of the republic, the story of Rome's Trojan origins was replaced by the older native tradition that Rome had been founded by colonists from Alba Longa. Romulus rather than Aeneas became accepted as the founder of the city and as *pater patriae*.

Some time in the late fourth century, the story of Aeneas was revived. The cult of the Dioscuri was reorganized so as to stress a connection with Aeneas; and it is fairly certain that, by 281 BC, when Pyrrhus crossed over into southern Italy, the Romans had once more accepted the tradition of their Trojan ancestry. We cannot be sure why this revival took place, but several possibilities suggest themselves. The decline of the Etruscan threat may, as Galinsky remarks, have rendered the Romans less averse to connection with an Etruscan founder-hero, and the protracted struggle with the Latin tribes stands to have lessened the Roman's enthusiasm for an exclusive Latin origin. Indeed, it is possible that, by reviving the legend of the Etruscan Aeneas, Rome announced that she had now taken the place which formerly belonged to Etruria. She had become the most powerful state in Italy. If the story of Aeneas originally signified Etruscan domination, its revival in the late fourth century might well be the expression of Rome's supremacy over Latium.[9]

But too direct a connection of Aeneas with the founding of Rome was bound to evoke unwelcome memories of Etruscan rule. Besides, the tradition of Rome's foundation by Latin colonists had now become too firmly established to be set aside, and the fact that Rome was taken to have been founded in the eighth century, some four hundred years after the fall of Troy, made it impossible to ascribe the foundation directly to a band of Trojan refugees. All these difficulties were overcome by making Aeneas the founder of Lavinium and the originator of the long line of Alban kings from which Romulus and Remus were eventually to spring. In this way, the legend of Aeneas was restored without making him the direct founder of the city, the chronological problem was solved, and a politically useful compromise was reached.[10] It is, according to Galinsky, this compromise that we find embodied in the fragments of Naevius and Fabius and in the annalists of the second century.

Unfortunately, Galinsky's thesis remains, in the end, an exercise in speculation based on scraps of archaeological evidence and fragments from Greek accounts of doubtful historical value. Even if Aeneas did figure in the public worship of Etruscan Rome, we have no way of knowing whether there was any myth attached, or, if there was, what form the myth took. The most we can say is that the story, as we have it in Naevius, first took shape in the third century when the expansion of Rome's power brought her into conflict with the Greek cities of the southern and eastern seaboards. Indeed, Perret has argued that the myth of Rome's Trojan origins was not explicitly formulated until the outbreak of the war with Pyrrhus. Pyrrhus, we know, prided himself on being the descendant of Achilles; and Pausanias tells us that when, in 281 BC, the Tarentine ambassadors appealed to him for aid in their struggle with Rome, he recalled the fall of Troy and hoped 'that he might repeat that victory, the descendant of Achilles fighting against a Trojan colony'.[11] Shortly afterwards, the Sicilian historian, Timaeus, examined the customs and religious practices of the Romans and found what he took to be proof that the Romans must indeed have come from Troy. His authority weighed heavily with other historians; and, according to Perret, it was thus that the story of Rome's Trojan origins was born and became an accepted fact, not only among the Greeks, but also at Rome.[12]

Perret's thesis has proved far too narrow to command general acceptance. Pausanias's notice conceals as much as it reveals; and it is, in any case, difficult to decide how seriously Pyrrhus himself took the precedent of the Trojan war. But the fact remains that Pyrrhus presented his expedition as a Greek crusade against the ancient Trojan enemy and that this is the first well-attested instance of the foundation myth being used in political argument.

Foundation and empire

Whatever the origin of the Aeneas story, its broad implications for the political awareness of the Roman people are plain. With their victory over Pyrrhus and the consolidation of their hegemony in Italy, the Romans had become a major power in the Mediterranean world. The need arose to give some account of their relationship to the Greek states in the east and to the empire of Carthage in the south. The story of Aeneas served the purpose admirably. By ascribing the foundation of Rome to the descendants of Trojan refugees, it gave the republic a place which would be immediately understood wherever Greek culture had penetrated.

The destruction of Troy had, by the fifth century, come to be seen as a crucial episode in the ancient feud between Asia and Europe, between East and West. It is by reference to this quarrel that Herodotus accounts for the Persian invasions of Greece, and Homer's *Iliad* may well have acquired its status as a national epic when the Persian threat led the Greeks to discover a common purpose in their struggle against the Asiatic barbarians. During and after the Peloponnesian Wars, the idea of a united Greece confronting the hordes of Asia lost much of its force in the city-states of the south; but it remained a living tradition in the northern kingdoms of Epirus and Macedon, and Alexander's conquests in Asia brought it once more to the fore. Alexander himself sought inspiration in the example of Achilles, and it appears that his expedition against Persia was widely recognized as a second Trojan war, a further episode in the perennial feud between East and West.[13]

The Romans, by tracing their origins to Troy, claimed for themselves a central role in this cosmic conflict. The young republic was Troy reborn. She had inherited the mantle of Asia and, with it, the enmity of the Greeks. Her destiny was to avenge the ancient wrong by reducing the Greeks to subjection.

The best evidence for the currency of this view is the way the Greek cities used the myth when circumstances made a reconciliation with Rome desirable. When, during the First Punic War, the citizens of Segesta staged their revolt against Carthage, they recalled a tradition to the effect that, like Rome, their own city had been founded by Trojan immigrants; and, thus, they smoothed the way for a convenient alliance.[14] Similarly, Strabo tells us that, after the First Punic War, the

Acarnanians appealed to Rome for help in their quarrel with the Aetolians, pleading that they alone of the Greeks had not taken part in the destruction of Troy.[15] In the years following the Second Punic War, many other Greek cities followed suit in exploiting the myth for diplomatic purposes. The task was not always easy. But the need for peace on favourable terms provided the motive, and the story of Aeneas's long and perilous voyage from Troy to Latium allowed for almost endless elaboration. As Perret has shown, many of the details concerning the hospitable reception Aeneas received at various places in Greece and Sicily were invented in the second century when the Greeks sought to adjust themselves to the growing power of Rome. From being an expression of implacable hostility, the myth had become, paradoxically, the ground on which a reconciliation could be effected.[16]

It is obvious enough that the story of Rome's Trojan origins made sense in the context of a war with the Greeks. But it is not so clear why the story should have received particular emphasis during the Second Punic War. Carthage was, like Rome, a city of supposedly Asiatic origin. According to the vendetta-logic of the myth, the two cities should, therefore, have been allies in a general confrontation with the Greeks. Yet it was precisely at the height of Rome's final struggle with Carthage that Naevius and Fabius chose to stress the Trojan origins of the Roman people.

It may well be that, by then, the story of Aeneas had become so firmly established as the national myth that it was retained with no thought for its implications when Rome became embroiled with Carthage. It is also possible that, in his epic, Naevius included the famous episode of Aeneas's visit to Carthage and his ill-starred love affair with the queen, Dido. In Virgil's later account, this episode is presented as the origin of the feud between Carthage and Rome, and we may suppose that it was originally invented to explain the Punic Wars.[17] But more important than any of these considerations is the fact that the claim to Trojan descent was capable of several interpretations and could be used for many, often contradictory purposes. The attitude of the Greeks to the Trojans had always been ambivalent. On the one hand, the Trojans were the ancient enemy, the archetypal barbarians; on the other, the tragic fate of Troy was the theme of the Greek national epic, and the Greeks were conscious of sharing with the Trojans a common past. There was even a tradition to the effect that the Trojans themselves were of Greek descent. In short, the story of Aeneas could be made to have pro-Greek implications and (it has been argued) it was these implications which the Romans exploited during the Punic Wars. They had, by this time, acquired enough Greek culture to think of their city as a centre of Hellenic civilization; and, by drawing attention to their Trojan origin, they explicitly invoked the Homeric past and declared themselves to be an integral part of the Greek world.[18]

But the myth had other implications which came to the fore in the aftermath of the Second Punic War. The claim to Trojan descent encouraged the notion that the Romans had a destiny to fulfil in Asia. We know of at least one occasion on which the Romans used their Trojan origins as an excuse for a diplomatic intervention in the affairs of the East.[19] And when, in 190 BC, L. Cornelius Scipio and P. Cornelius Scipio Africanus went to Asia Minor, they took pains to visit Troy and greet the inhabitants as kinsmen of the Roman people.[20] Moreover, the achievement of Alexander had given substance to the idea that the ancient conflict between Europe and Asia was fated to end with the establishment of a universal empire. Having emerged victorious from the second and decisive struggle with Carthage, Rome had become the dominant power in the then known world; and many Romans came to regard their republic as having inherited Alexander's project.[21]

There is no evidence that either Naevius or Fabius had a clear conception of Rome's imperial destiny. But Polybius is our witness that, by the middle of the century, this destiny had become manifest. 'Previously,' he tells us, 'the doings of the world had been, so to say, dispersed, as they were held together by no unity of initiative, results or locality.' But now, with the fall of Carthage and the defeat of Philip and Antiochus in the East, it became possible to see how all that had gone before had conspired to produce a single momentous result, namely, the domination of 'nearly the whole inhabited World' by a single state, 'a thing unique in history'.[22] During the latter half of the century the Romans became accustomed to thinking of themselves as the lords of the world. In 82 BC, a globe, signifying world-wide power, appeared on the coinage of Sulla; and, by the time of Cicero, it was common form to describe the territory controlled by Rome as 'the whole world', *orbis terrarum*.[23]

The achievement (or near prospect) of universal empire cast a new light on the traditions the Romans had preserved concerning their past. Once men knew the end as well as the beginning of the story, all the intervening details fell into place. It now became possible to highlight the points that were relevant and to eliminate those that were not. The past, in short, was revised to make it coherent with the present.

The main outlines of this reconstruction can be traced to Fabius Pictor himself. In the annalistic tradition he founded, early Rome is consistently presented as having been, from the beginning, an autonomous city-state and, indeed, the dominant power in the plain of Latium. The true importance of the neighbouring cities, Lavinium and Alba Longa, is concealed, and virtually all memory of the Etruscan conquest is suppressed.[24] There is no reason to suppose that Fabius deliberately distorted the facts. He wrote, not as an objective historian, but as a patriotic citizen who held the unshakeable belief that, despite the holocaust at Cannae, Rome was invincible and could not but emerge victorious. Any reports of the past which conflicted with this undoubted fact must therefore be false. Rome might well have met with set-backs before, but never with ultimate defeat.

The successful outcome of the Second Punic War only served to confirm the view that Rome was destined never to be overcome. The republic, it was said, would stand so long as a single togaed Roman remained.[25] The temporary defeats inflicted by Carthaginians, Gauls and Samnites were merely so much evidence for the truth of the great lesson conveyed by the foundation myth itself. Rome was, as Ennius put it, 'Troy's citadel which on the plain of Dardanus could not perish or be made captive when captured or when burnt become ashes.' (*Ann.*, 349–50.)

Polybius, in his *History*, had ascribed the success of Rome to the excellence of her constitution and the discipline of her armies. However, Ennius and his like were more inclined to seek an explanation in the act of foundation. Romulus had, by his deeds, established the identity of the Roman people. Before the foundation, men had lived, worked and died in much the same way as they did afterwards. But they were not Romans. They lacked the political existence, the corporate identity, which only the city could provide. Just as men owed their biological existence to their natural parents, so they owed their political existence to the city of which they were citizens. In this sense, the founder of the city was the 'father and begetter' who 'brought us forth into the world of light'. (*Ann.*, 117–21.) But, above all, the foundation had established the character of the Romans as a people, and it was in terms of their character that they explained their rise to greatness.

In Latin literature we find it repeatedly stressed that the proper standard of behaviour, both public and private, is the *mos maiorum*, the customs or morals of the ancestors. It is true that considerable importance was attached to the supernatural aspects of the foundation. The founders themselves had been descendants of the gods, and the future destiny of the city had been decreed by Fate. In his *De natura deorum* (III, ii, 5) Cicero has the venerable Cotta declare that 'Romulus by his auspices and Numa by the establishment of our ritual laid the foundations of our state which certainly could never have attained its present greatness had it not fully propitiated the immortal gods.' But, for the most part, it was assumed that the fulfilment of Rome's destiny in the future depended on the people continuing to display the virtues by which that destiny had been accomplished in the past. The old standards of behaviour and the institutions which encouraged them had, therefore, to be preserved. The deeds and characters of great Romans in the past became precedents to guide the conduct of men in the present. As Ennius put, it: 'On men and on manners of olden time stands firm the Roman state.' (*Ann.*, 467.) And the most powerful precedents of all were those established by Romulus himself. Whether the Republic was being 'restored to its ancient state' or merely 'preserved', it was the acts of Romulus that were endlessly repeated. The founder hero was merely the first in a long line of fathers and begetters. Camillus and Marius were both, in their time, declared to be the second founders of the city and were likened to Romulus; and, after his suppression of Catiline's conspiracy, Cicero himself was hailed as *parens patriae*, father of his country.

The dilemma of the Roman ruling class

We now turn to the uses Romans made of their myth in dealing with the internal problems that emerged during the waning years of the republic. These problems were primarily of an economic and social nature. But they were conceived in terms of the political ethic of the Roman nobility; and it is this ethic which we must briefly explain.

In all practical thinking which is not merely technical in character, we find a preoccupation with the idea of achieving a morally coherent world. This preoccupation manifests itself in various ways; but, generally, it comes to the fore when, in their practical experience, men discover a conflict between themselves as individuals and the natural and social world in which they live. In Rome, at the time of Ennius, this conflict found expression in the opposition of virtue and fortune, a theme which recurs in virtually every writer of the period whose works have survived. Usually, the term *fortuna* signifies the prospect of unforeseen disaster that dogs the footsteps of the individual. A sudden storm may wreck his ships, an unseasonable drought may blight his crops, war or disease may bring untimely death. 'In no wise,' says Ennius, 'has fortune followed any man all his days.' (*Ann.*, 286.) The problem, it appears, was not the magnitude of the disasters that fortune might bring but the fact that, since these disasters struck with no regard for the merit of the individual, they were unpredictable. Thus Ennius has Antiochus complain of 'fortune who has bruised me and destroyed me in fierce and bitter war—and I deserved it not'. (*Ann.*, 381–2.) From the standpoint of the individual, a world in which fortune operated was a hostile, arbitrary and ultimately alien world. It was a morally incoherent world in which a man's most reasonable expectations might be frustrated and both the virtuous and the wicked were struck down with shocking impartiality. The world, in brief, was radically unjust.

Stoicism provided a solution of sorts, but, though fashionable in educated circles, it did not become a popular creed. The common people preferred to seek consolation in mystic doctrines according to which man is a mere sojourner or pilgrim hastening through this world to his true home in the next. And, on the whole, the nobles rejected both Stoic *contemptus mundi* and the apocalyptic visions of the mystics to find the fulfilment of their hopes in the political life of the old republic.

One of the distinguishing features of life in the city-state was the sharp distinction its citizens drew between the public and the private.[26] Each citizen was recognized as having two spheres of activity. On the one hand, there were those activities which had to do with his economic and family interests and which concerned him alone. On the other, there were those activities which concerned the community as a whole and which he performed in public, before the eyes of his fellow-citizens. At Rome, there was no doubt which of these two spheres was the most important. It was the public sphere. It was on the public stage, and there alone, that the citizen could demonstrate his worth and win distinction in the eyes of his peers. And he did so by performing acts aimed at achieving the public good. As Donald Earl has put it, the virtue of the Roman citizen 'consisted in the winning of personal preeminence and glory by the commission of great deeds in the service of the Roman state'.[27]

As in many other city-states, it was understood that only those who had sufficient property to be secure in the satisfaction of their needs were qualified for citizenship. The reason for this was two-fold. It was supposed, firstly, that those who had property would take an interest in maintaining the state that protected it; and, secondly, it was thought that no man would act for the common good if poverty compelled him to consider his private interest first. The purpose of property, in short, was not simply to make a man rich but to make him a citizen and thus to open the door for a political career.

Of course, the possession of property did not exempt a man from the blows of fortune. On the contrary, it exposed him to particular risk in that it entailed an obligation to serve in the army. However, though death in battle might seem the ultimate victory of fortune over the individual, this victory was, for the Roman citizen, cancelled out by the glory he achieved through his deeds; for glory conferred upon the individual a life that did not perish with his mortal body. Of this the Romans were almost obsessively aware. Naevius, for instance, describes M. Claudius Marcellus as returning to Rome after his victory at Clastidium, 'happy in life never dying'. (*Clast.*) Cicero tells us that 'among all the rewards of virtue, if rewards must be taken into account, the noblest is glory; this alone is enough to compensate for life's brevity by the remembrance of future ages, to make us present in absence and alive in death'. (*Pro Milone*, 97.) And Sallust, after remarking on the shortness of life, declares that if only men would put their virtue to use, they 'would attain to that height of greatness where from mortals their glory would make them immortal'. (*Iug.*, 5.)

In the Roman tradition, a virtue which was not exercised, or was exercised only in the obscurity of private life, was no virtue at all. It passed unseen, unrecorded and unremembered. To become real, virtue required more than simply to be translated into action; it had also to achieve public recognition, for, only in so far as a man's virtue was acknowledged by others did it attain an existence independent of his own private self-appreciation. Of course, the public before whose eyes the citizen performed his deeds and which awarded glory was narrowly circumscribed. It was the ruling class itself, and not the mob, whose judgement was the standard of excellence. Cicero thus defines glory as 'praise given to right action and the reputation for great merits in the service of the republic which is approved not merely by the testimony of the multitude but by the witness of all the best men'. (*Pro Sestio*, 139.) Unlike fame which might vanish with any change in popular mood, glory was to stand for all time.

It is not difficult to understand the value the Roman nobility attached to their political life. To be denied citizenship was to be excluded from the public sphere and thus to be condemned to obscurity and a kind of living death. It was the despised condition of slaves, women and strangers. By making the safety of the people his personal concern, the Roman citizen achieved, in his practice, an identification of himself with the community of which he was a part. He became a public person. In a sense, he had no life of his own. The life he lived was the life of the city. What he did in the public sphere had a place and a significance in a world that was greater and more permanent than himself. His fortune as a mere individual might be capricious and unpredictable. But the destiny of the republic was not, and the republic was embodied in each of its citizens. In his service to the state, the citizen abandoned the incoherent world of private life and entered the harmonious realm of public affairs where his achievements would win him a life never dying.

By the time of Cicero, it had become clear that the political practices and institutions of the republic were in danger of collapse. The republic which had, in the third century, defeated Pyrrhus still bore some resemblance to a typical city-state. After a protracted struggle, the plebeians had won first citizenship and then access to public office. The resolutions of the plebs in the tribal assemblies, the *comitia tributa*, had acquired the force of law; and the annual magistrates, elected by the people, performed the task of routine administration and provided the nobility with a well-defined *cursus honorum*. The citizen-body itself consisted, in the main, of small farmers. They worked the land, paid the taxes and, in times of war, they did military service under the command of their elected magistrates.

The difficulties which beset this republic in the years following the Second Punic War had their root in the chronic inability of the small farmer to maintain his position. Bad harvests and the burdens of taxation and military service led, as often as not, to debt and eventually to dispossession. From the earliest times, the tendency was for the rich to grow richer and for the poor to become poorer and the Punic Wars only served to accelerate the process. The newly conquered territories either paid tax in kind or were added to the public domain for exploitation by the rich. The advantages of large agricultural estates worked by slave labour soon became apparent; and, before long, Rome ceased to be economically dependent on the labour of her own citizens. Those Italian farmers who had survived the ravages of war now found themselves in hopeless competition with cheap grain imported from the provinces. They abandoned their farms and fled to the city to swell the ranks of the urban proletariat.

Herein lay the predicament that faced the Roman nobility. Since their new-found wealth was derived from their exploitation of the conquered territories, they had an obvious interest in the maintenance of the empire. However, the maintenance of the empire depended on military power, and, with the depopulation of the Italian countryside, the number of citizens eligible for military service was steadily declining. Slaves could not be armed, and landless mercenaries were unreliable.

A possible solution to the problem was to redistribute the public domain and to fix a limit to the amount of land any one citizen might hold. Indeed, measures of this kind were proposed first by the tribune,

Flaminius, and later (in 133 BC) by Tiberius Gracchus. Attempts at agrarian reform enjoyed considerable popular support, but they met with violent opposition from those whose estates were put in jeopardy, namely, the *equites* and the senatorial nobility. Furthermore, the tactics adopted by Tiberius Gracchus provoked a constitutional crisis which was to trouble the republic for years to come. Thanks largely to its successful conduct of the Punic Wars, the Senate had acquired powers that were not strictly constitutional. Control of finance and foreign policy had become its prerogative and, by the beginning of the second century, it had replaced the *comitia tributa* as the main source of law. Faced with the opposition of the Senate, Tiberius Gracchus revived the dormant legislative powers of the *comitia*. His reforms, though never implemented, did become law, and the lesson was not lost on the politically ambitious. Henceforth, the ruling class was divided between those who sought power through the tribal assemblies and those who strove to maintain the authority of the Senate.[28]

Associated with the issue of agrarian reform was the problem of Rome's deteriorating relationships with her Italian allies. The Italian communities had supplied a large proportion of the men and the money with which Rome fought her wars. Now, towards the end of the second century, they began to press for a share in political power. Defenders of the old order, men such as Cato, were fiercely opposed to any extension of citizenship rights, and senatorial obstruction prevailed until, in 90 BC, the Italians staged a general revolt. The revolt was crushed, but with the utmost difficulty and only after the Romans had conceded the rights of citizenship to many of the Italian communities.

The inclusion of the Italians was, no doubt, a necessary step. But it did not halt the erosion of the economic and social foundations of the old republic and neither did it solve the political difficulties of the Roman nobility. In the days when the hegemony of Rome was confined to central Italy, political power had rested firmly in the hands of the citizen body and its elected magistrates. But all this had now changed. From being an economically self-sufficient community of farmers and soldiers, Rome had become a large urban centre dependent for its livelihood on the exploitation of distant provinces. Increasingly, the defence of the empire required the granting of extraordinary powers to popular military commanders. Effective power was transferred from the Senate and people of Rome to the men who controlled the provinces and commanded the professional soldiers who, by now, had replaced the old citizen army. The nobility needed these men to protect its economic interests, but it feared them, for it had, in the last resort, no way of curbing their ambition except by playing the one off against the other. The Roman people itself had become a landless rabble quick to riot but unable to fight. And, as the major public offices lost all significance—apart from being the stepping-stone to military power—political life degenerated into violence and electoral corruption. In short, the Roman nobility found itself in the unhappy position of being able to maintain its economic power only at the risk of forfeiting its political position.

Cicero's version of the Foundation Myth

We must now examine the way in which the dilemma of the Roman nobility was reflected in the second book of Cicero's *Republic*, the earliest account of Rome's origin to survive in more than fragmentary form. Cicero, we find, quotes extensively from Ennius's *Annales* and, further, he makes it clear that he has modelled his account of Rome's foundation on Cato's *Origines*. However, his version differs from that of his two predecessors in one important respect. He makes no mention of Aeneas, and he nowhere refers to the Trojan origins of the Roman people. Instead, he begins his account directly with the birth of Romulus. There can be little doubt that the omission was deliberate; but what did it signify?

It is possible that, by the time of Cicero (i.e. first century BC), the anti-Greek implications of Rome's Trojan origins had ceased to serve any useful purpose. Rome had long since established her dominion over the Greeks, and the Greek cities were, on the whole, content to have exchanged a tenuous independence for the benefits of imperial protection. Memories of the ancient feud between Greek and Trojan could only serve to disturb the peace. And the other implications of the myth may well have become equally embarrassing. The Aeneas legend had, we recall, placed Rome firmly in the orbit of Hellenic civilization and had held out the promise of an imperial destiny in the East. But the conservative nobility at Rome had, from the beginning, resisted the influx of new ideas and practices from overseas; and, though the expansion of Roman power into Asia met with general approval, it also caused a certain amount of apprehension. The Eastern provinces were far more wealthy, populous and cultured than anything found in the West, and many Romans must have sensed that Rome's position as the natural centre and capital of the empire was now in the balance. Indeed Suetonius reports that, after the defeat of Pompey, Caesar was accused of wishing to transfer the capital either to Alexandria or to Troy. (*Caes*, I, XXIX.) The accusation may not have been justified, but it shows that, by the middle of the century, many Romans had found in the story of Aeneas the unwelcome implication that Rome should one day return to her place of origin. An insistence on a strictly Latin origin would underline the point that Latium was irrevocably the home and seat of Roman power and that Rome owed her greatness to those qualities which were peculiarly her own. Cicero, certainly, goes out of his way to emphasize the political importance of Rome's geographical position. And, despite his admiration for the literary achievements of the Greeks, he tailors his account to show 'that we Romans got our culture, not from arts imported from overseas, but from the native genius and virtue of our own people'. (*Rep.*, II, 29.)

The Romans had also to adjust themselves to the consequences of their recent policy in Italy. Earlier versions of the myth had tended to stress the Romans' awareness of themselves as a people apart. Their Trojan origin made them aliens in Italy, and there was a tradition that Romulus had increased the population of his city by making it a haven for outlaws and refugees.[29] The revolt of the Italian allies in 90 BC had compelled the Romans to recognize their neighbours and former enemies in the peninsula as fellow citizens, but bad feeling still remained on both sides. The story of Romulus with its implication that the Romans were of good Italian stock would help reconcile the disgruntled Italians, and convincing precedents were found to allay the suspicions of conservative nobles at Rome. As Cicero remarks: 'What has undoubtedly done most to establish our empire and to increase the renown of the Roman people is that Romulus, that first founder of this city, taught us by the treaty which he made with the Sabines that this state ought to be enlarged by the admission of even enemies as citizens. Through his authority and example, our forefathers never ceased to grant and bestow citizenship.' (*Pro Balbo*, 31.)

These are some of the reasons which might have induced Cicero to suppress the story of Aeneas. However, Cicero himself did not explain his omission, and any inferences we might draw from his known views or from the climate of opinion which (we suppose) prevailed at his time are nothing but speculation. Forunately, we find ourselves on firmer ground when we turn to the positive content of Cicero's account.

After a brief description of Romulus's birth and upbringing, Cicero goes on to discuss the foundation of the city, and here his main concern is to stress the remarkable foresight—*providentia*—Romulus displayed in choosing the site. He 'perceived that a site on the sea-coast is not the most desirable for cities founded in the hope of long life and extended dominion'. (*Rep.*, II, 5.) As Cicero explains, cities on the seaboard are exposed to sudden attack and often find it difficult to maintain their ancestral institutions intact because they are subject to the influence of foreign customs; their citizens, drawn to the sea, abandon agriculture and the pursuit of arms; and trade brings inducements to luxury and indolence. On the other hand, he notes, an agricultural community must be able to trade its surplus produce for the products of other cities. The best possible site for a city is, therefore, an inland position by the banks of a navigable river. And it was such a site that Romulus chose. 'Consequently,' says Cicero, 'it seems to me that Romulus must at the very beginning have divined that the city would one day be the seat and hearthstone of a mighty empire; for scarcely could a city placed upon any other site in Italy have more easily maintained our present widespread power.' (*Rep.*, II, 10.)

This, then, was why Cicero regarded the act of foundation as being of special significance. In his view, Rome's destiny was (at least in part) determined by her geographical position, and she owed her geographical position to the remarkable foresight of her founder. But the significance of his act was limited. Romulus had, indeed, laid the grounds for Rome's future greatness but he had done no more than that. Rome's position in the world was assured only when the city had achieved a complete political existence, a perfect *res publica*; and this achievement was, Cicero insists, the work of many generations. 'Cato,' he tells us, 'used to say that our constitution was superior to those of other states because almost every one of these other commonwealths had been established by one man. . . . But our own commonwealth was based upon the genius, not of one man, but of many; it was founded, not in one generation, but in a long period of several centuries and many ages of men.' (*Rep.*, II, 2.)

Cicero now illustrates the point by describing the reforms which the various kings of Rome introduced. Romulus, having united the Romans and the Sabines into one community, established the Senate, for he recognized the principle that the state can be better governed by the power of a king 'if the authority of the state's most eminent men is joined to the ruler's absolute power'. (*Rep.*, II, 15.) He also gave complete obedience to the auspices, 'a custom which we still observe to the great security of the state', (*Rep.*, II, 16), and instituted the college of augurs. After his death, the Roman people demanded a new king. Perceiving that 'kingly virtue and wisdom, not royal ancestry, were the qualities to be sought', (*Rep.*, II, 24), they chose the Sabine, Numa Pompilius, and had his election confirmed by a curiate law. Numa divided up among the citizens the lands which Romulus had won by conquest, 'and showed them that by the cultivation of their farms they could have an abundance of all manner of possessions, without resort to pillage or plunder'. (*Rep.*, II, 26.) In this way, he implanted a love for peace and tranquillity and enabled justice and good faith to flourish. His other reforms had the same effect. 'By the introduction of religious ceremonial, through laws which still remain on our records, he quenched the people's ardour for the warlike life to which they had been accustomed.' (*Rep.*, II, 26.) And, by the institution of markets, games and other occasions for social intercourse, he encouraged the habits of benevolence and kindliness.

The third king, Tullius Hostilius, followed the precedent of Numa in having the people confirm his election in the curiate assembly. He was, however, a great military leader. From the proceeds of his spoils, he built a meeting-place for the popular assemblies, and he formulated rules for the declaration of war. The reign of the fourth king, Ancus Marcius, was marked chiefly by the introduction of Greek learning and culture; but his successor, Lucius Tarquinius, reformed and enlarged the Senate and established the order of knights, the *equites*. He also instituted the Roman games and built the temple of Jupiter on the Capitoline Hill. Finally, the sixth king, Servius Tullius, established the centuriate assembly, working on the principle that, while no one should be deprived of the suffrage, the majority of the votes should go to the men of property for whom the welfare of the state was most important. (*Rep.*, II, 31–41.)

This process of piecemeal reform gradually brought the constitution nearer perfection. As Laelius complacently remarks, 'Now we have further proof of the accuracy of Cato's statement that the foundation of our republic was the work neither of one period nor of one man; for it is quite clear that every king contributed many good and useful institutions.' (*Rep.*, II, 37.) However, the abiding defect of Rome's early monarchical constitution was, in Cicero's view, its instability. He concedes that the monarchy found room for aristocratic and democratic modes of procedure, but, he argues, the three elements were so combined that there was no true balance between them. The ultimate power rested in the hands of one man for life, and, so long as this remained, the monarchy could be transformed into a tyranny, not through the king seizing any new powers, but by his misuse of the powers he already possessed. 'The fortune of any people is therefore a fragile thing . . . when it depends on the will or the character of one man.' (*Rep.*, II, 50.)

With the tyranny of Tarquinius Superbus, the fortune of the Roman people duly failed. The senators, led by Brutus, expelled the Tarquins and put in their place two consuls elected annually. This was a major step towards stability but not the final step. As Cicero points out, the government was so administered 'that, though the people were free, few political acts were performed by them, practically everything being done by the authority of the senate and in accordance with its established customs, and that the consuls held a power which, though only of one year's duration, was truly regal in general character and in legal sanction.' (*Rep.*, II, 56.) The government, in short, was essentially aristocratic with an element of monarchical power. It therefore fell short of perfection, for 'unless there is in the state an even balance of rights, duties and functions so that the magistrates have enough power, the counsels of the eminent citizens enough authority and the people enough liberty, this kind of government cannot be safe from revolution'. (*Rep.*, II, 57.) Accordingly, in the sixteenth year of the republic, 'an event occurred which in the nature of things was bound to happen: the people, freed from the domination of kings, claimed a somewhat greater measure of rights'. (*Rep.*, II, 57.) After a brief conflict, the plebeian tribunes were established to counterbalance the power of the consuls and to keep the authority of the Senate in check. The constitution of the republic was now complete, and with this Cicero concludes his account. But what was it all intended to convey?

For the Roman nobility, the merit of the old republican constitution was that it provided a public platform on which men of outstanding ability could vie with one another for the prize of glory. The eventuality they most feared was that the state might fall into the hands of a faction or of one man, for this would end the contest and deprive the citizen of the glory due to his merit. 'Kings,' as Sallust points out, 'hold the good in greater suspicion than the wicked and to them the virtue of others is fraught with danger.' (*Cat.*, vii.) Although Cicero finds much to be said for the rule of a wise and benevolent king, he insists that any monarchy is inherently weak and that even the best of monarchies lacks the basic prerequisite of a political life, namely, liberty 'which does not consist in serving a just master but in serving no master at all'. (*Rep.*, II, 43.)

In the old republic, detestation of monarchy was such that the people 'could not bear even to hear the title of king mentioned'. (*Rep.*, II, 52.) However, by the time of Cicero, popular hostility to kingship had declined into curiosity. Scipio Africanus had suffered from comparing himself with Alexander the Great, but Pompey did so explicitly and with success. When Caesar marched on Rome, the nobles, whose cause Cicero championed, were left in no doubt as to the danger that faced them. We cannot tell whether Caesar really intended to make himself king; but we know that many Romans suspected the worst and that their suspicions were nourished by his declared wish to extend Rome's dominions in the East. It was clear that Egypt could be held in subjection only by a divine king of the kind the Egyptians were accustomed to obey. And, according to a rumour current in Rome, the Sibylline books had predicted that the Parthians would never submit to the Romans until the latter should be commanded by a king. At the time of his assassination, Caesar was, in fact, planning a campaign against Parthia, and the Senate was reported to be ready to grant him royal powers for the purpose. Cicero himself was convinced that Caesar intended to restore the monarchy and said so on several occasions. And, although the *Republic* was written a few years before Caesar emerged as the sole ruler of Rome, its anti-monarchical import is unmistakable.[30]

The Romans, we recall, regarded themselves as bound by the *mos majorum* and, in particular, by the precedents established by the founders of their city. The city Romulus founded was, of course, a monarchy, and the implications of this were not lost on men such as Caesar. Early in his career, Caesar had pointedly traced the origins of the Julian *gens* to its roots in the royal line established by Aeneas; later, he invited comparison with Romulus by claiming the right to offer the *spolia maxima* and by allowing his statue to be placed alongside the statues of the ancient kings.[31] Cicero was equally aware of the uses to which the precedent of Romulus might be put, and his account of Rome's foundation was designed as a counterblast. The point is nothing if not explicit. Romulus had launched the founding of the city but had not completed it. He was merely the first of many founders. Not until the monarchy had been abolished and the liberty of the people secured by the power of the tribunes was the foundation complete. And it was this foundation, not that of Romulus, which embodied the authentic achievement of the fathers.

As we have seen, the Romans regarded death as the most striking manifestation of fortune's power. In Book III of his *Republic*, Cicero remarks that, although death is inevitable for individuals, there is nothing either natural or necessary in the destruction of a state, 'for a state ought to be so firmly founded that it will live for ever'. (*Rep.*, III, 34.) Developing a theory (borrowed from Polybius) Cicero argues that the three primary forms of state all suffer from inherent defects which must, sooner or later, bring about their destruction. Monarchies inevitably degenerate into tyranny, aristocracies become dominated by oligarchical factions and democracy is all too easily converted into mob-rule. But a mixed constitution, in which the three primary forms of state are combined to make an even balance, can sustain itself indefinitely.[32] And Rome, in Cicero's view, was just such a state. This is not to say that nothing the Romans did could possibly jeopardize the continued existence of their commonwealth. Rome would last only so long as the people maintained their ancestral institutions intact and continued to display the virtues exemplified by their forefathers.[33] The destiny of Rome was not guaranteed but—and this is Cicero's point—it was placed within the power of the people themselves to control. Thanks to their foundation, their collective fortune depended entirely on their virtue.

In Cicero's view, the Romans of his day had conspicuously failed to maintain the standard set by the rustic heroes of the old republic. Where, he enquires, are the morals on which, according to Ennius, the Roman state stands firm? 'They are scarcely even to be found in books; even the records which told of that old-fashioned sternness are no more to be seen.' (*Pro Cael.*, 40.) The Romans, he declares have only themselves to blame. 'For it is through our own faults, and not by any accident, that we retain the republic in name but have long since lost it in actual fact.' (*Rep.*, V, 2.)

The theme was a common one, and there was a measure of agreement that the decline in morals had something to do with the empire. Sallust tells us that, when the republic had grown great through toil and justice and the defeat of Carthage had opened the road to world dominion, 'then fortune began to grow cruel and to bring confusion into all our affairs'. (*Cat.*, x.) The conquered territories offered temptations which the Romans were ill-prepared to resist. The lust for power and then for money grew upon them till 'finally, when the disease had spread like a deadly plague, the state was changed and a government second to none in equity and excellence became cruel and intolerable'. (ibid.) Later historians, such as Livy and Velleius Paterculus, also linked the decline of the republic with the growth of the empire; and Appian, in Book I of his *The Civil Wars*, provided a remarkably perceptive analysis of the way the acquisition of overseas territories and the depopulation of the Italian countryside determined the breakdown of political life at Rome.

Cicero's stand-point was slightly different. The argument with which he was mainly concerned was the moral one that no state can acquire dominion over others without committing injustice and thereby corrupting its own political life. To this, the aged statesman, Laelius, is made to give a detailed reply. Most of his discourse is lost, but we know it contained the points that Rome won her empire exclusively by just wars fought in defence of her allies, that, in any case, dominion is justified where the rulers are superior in virtue to their subjects, and that the Romans of the old republic vindicated their right to rule by the probity with which they conducted their affairs. Power, in short, does not corrupt. On the contrary, the maintenance of power depends precisely on a strict adherence to the precepts of justice, and where justice is abandoned, as it was at Rome, then power itself is put at risk. 'If,' he concludes, 'this habit of lawlessness begins to spread and changes our rule from one of justice to one of force, so that those who up to now have obeyed us willingly are held faithful by fear alone, then, though our own generation has perhaps been vigilant enough to be safe, yet I am anxious for our descendants, and for the immortality of our republic which might live on for ever if the institutions and morals of our ancestors were maintained.' (*Rep.*, III, 41.)

In one respect, Cicero's line of argument is entirely mythical. The Roman people have a glorious task to perform, but they can do so only if they remain faithful to their character; and their character as a people was established by the deeds of the men who founded the republic. All hope for the future rests on the people being able to recover their lost identity. How this recovery is to be achieved Cicero does not say. We may surmise that he envisaged some sort of second foundation or return to the origins.

But, in another respect, Cicero's account of the foundation is more than merely a myth. The bare bones of the story are there, but they are fleshed out with a mass of theoretical and historical discussion. The epic poets had simply told the tale. To their minds, the greatness of Rome was adequately explained and justified by reference to various prophecies which declared it to be the will of Fate. Otherwise, the story spoke for itself. By contrast, Cicero's narrative has all the trappings of a critical historical investigation. He carefully cites the records, both Greek and Roman, and digresses from time to time to make a chronological or etymological point. The technical merits and demerits of various constitutional innovations are minutely discussed. And, above all, the achievement of world dominion is explained in terms of Rome's advantageous geographical position, the moral qualities of her people, and the stability of the mixed constitution she had evolved. It is as if Cicero wished to reassert the values the myth had tended to promote but felt that the myth, by itself, was not sufficient to do the job. He therefore gave its implications additional support by drawing freely from the historical and philosophical culture of his time. In short, he rationalized the myth and, in so doing, he transformed it into an ideological statement.

The settlement of Augustus Caesar

Cicero was not alone in his stubborn adherence to the obsolete ideals of the republican nobility. Some of the nobles were, of course, happy enough to abandon a political life that had now become empty, but many chose to compete, by suicide or by death in battle, for the honour of being remembered as 'the last of the Romans'.

The settlement which Augustus made after his victory at Actium was generally hailed as *res publica redditta* or *res publica restituta*.[34] Augustus himself was compared to Romulus and acknowledged the comparison by having his statue placed in the temple of Quirinus, the founder deified. Indeed, it has been suggested that his title, Augustus, was not unconnected with Ennius's dictum that Romulus founded the city in 'august augury'.[35] In his own *Res Gestae*, Augustus presented his case in terms calculated to evoke republican ideals. Thus, he opens by declaring that: 'At the age of nineteen . . . I raised an army by means of which I restored liberty to the republic, which had been oppressed by the tyranny of a faction.' (*Res Gestae*, 1.) Further on, he protests that: 'I refused to accept any power offered me which was contrary to the traditions of our ancestors.' (ibid., 6.) And elsewhere he says, 'By the passage of new laws I restored many traditions of our ancestors which were then falling into disuse, and I myself set precedents in many things for posterity to imitate.' (ibid., 8.) But the stress which his followers placed on the extreme antiquity of the republic that was being restored left little doubt as to what had happened. For all practical purposes, a monarchy had been established. The popular assemblies were soon reduced to acclaiming the acts of the emperor and sanctioning his seizure of extraordinary powers; the authority of the Senate was replaced by the more weighty authority of Caesar; and, in time, it became clear that the proper arena for service to the state had been transferred from the forum to the imperial entourage.

In these circumstances, it is hardly surprising that the foundation myth as formulated by Naevius and revised by Cicero was revised yet again; and the *locus classicus* for this revision is Virgil's *Aeneid*.

I have already mentioned the major innovation introduced by Virgil, namely, the story of Dido and Aeneas. This episode gave the Punic Wars a crucial place in the tale of Rome's rise to universal empire. Peace and order could not be established in the civilized world until all ancient feuds had been settled, and so bitter was the feud with Carthage that it could admit of no compromise or reconciliation. If Rome were to achieve her destined end, Carthage had to be destroyed. It has also been argued that Virgil intended the episode of Dido and Aeneas to stand in edifying comparison with the notorious alliance between Antony and Cleopatra. In the eyes of many Romans, Antony's Eastern policy had marked him as a renegade, and Augustus was not slow to depict himself as leading the forces of Italy and the West against the dark, undisciplined and licentious hordes of the East. Antony, according to the official propaganda, had abandoned his ancestral gods and the customs of his forefathers to make himself the slave of an Oriental harlot. Aeneas, by contrast, had piously abandoned an African queen to conduct his people and his household gods to their home on the banks of the Tiber.[36]

Aeneas, in Virgil's epic, is the epitome of everything that is sober, decent and Roman. Above all, his achievement serves as an assurance that Rome, the capital of the West, shall forever hold sway over the lands of the East. The battle of Actium is merely the fulfilment of this guarantee. It is true that the story of Rome's Trojan origins could be taken to have quite different connotations, but Virgil knew how to bend his narrative to suit his purpose. When the Trojans reach their destination, they are greeted by King Latinus, who diplomatically recalls that, according to legend, Latium was the birthplace of Dardanus, the supposed founder of Troy. (*Aen.*, VII, 205.) So far from being alien interlopers, Aeneas and his followers are native sons of the soil returning to the land of their origin. And, towards the end of the poem, when Juno at last abandons her hostility to the Trojans, she exacts from Jupiter a significant concession. 'Command not the Latins, in a land which is their own, to change their ancient name, to become Trojans, or to be called Teucrians; command none to speak a different tongue or wear another garb. . . . Troy has fallen, and fallen permit her and her name to stay.' (*Aen.*, XII, 823.) The point could hardly be made more plain. Rome's existence depends on one condition: that the Roman people commit themselves to a distinctively Italian identity and dismiss forever all thoughts of restoring their seat of power in the East.

Virgil's attitude to the Greeks is more ambivalent. He does indeed stress the welcome support the Trojans received from Evander's Arcadian colony in Latium, but his account of Aeneas's flight from Troy is thick with references to the undying enmity between Trojan and Greek. And, at the very beginning of his poem, Jupiter is made to declare that 'an age shall come, as the years glide by, when the children of Troy shall enslave the children of Agamemnon, of Diomedes and Achilles and shall rule in conquered Argos'. (*Aen.*, I, 283.) On the other hand, Virgil's learned contemporary, Dionysius of Halicarnassus, leaves nothing undone in his effort to Hellenize the Romans. We have already encountered Dionysius in connection with the Euhemerist theory of myth, and we recall that he had set himself the task of proving that the Romans, so far from being barbarians, were of undiluted Greek extraction. In this enterprise, his interpretation of the story of Hercules and Cacus was far from his most striking achievement. Indeed, after arguing that the population of old Latium was composed partly of Arcadians and partly of Pelasgians from Thessaly, he rounds off his case by showing that even 'the Trojans were a nation as truly Greek as any and formerly came from the Peloponnesus'. (*Dion.*, I, lxi.) He all but tells us that the Roman empire is the old dream of a united Hellas fulfilled.

There is another point which many commentators have remarked upon. Cicero, we remember, had endorsed the republican view that glory is the proper reward of virtue, but he had qualified his remark with the phrase, 'if rewards must be taken into account'. This hint of doubt runs throughout his work. In part, it stems from his adherence to the Stoic doctrine that virtue, properly understood, is its own reward; in part, it is inspired by his fear that an unrestrained pursuit of individual glory might degenerate into a ruthless struggle for power. Virgil, as Donald Earl points out, associates glory with virtue only once, and that in a context that links it also with tyrannical arrogance. 'Aeneas, though amply qualified by his honourable birth and his fame which had mounted to heaven, lacks, precisely and deliberately, *gloria* and *nobilitas*. His great quality, emphasized and invoked at every turn of the poem, is *pietas*. It means nothing else than doing his duty to his gods, his country and his family.'[37] The empire, after years of civil war, looked for unity and peace, not for conflict; and, above all, the emperor required faithful servants, not rivals.

But perhaps the strongest impression the reader is likely to derive from Virgil's *Aeneid* is that Rome's future greatness was predestined from the very beginning. Aeneas himself is continually pictured as the willing instrument of a providential purpose. Always it is the 'call of fate' or the 'fateful purpose of the gods' that govern his action and sustain his revolve.[38] Time and again the promise of universal empire is confirmed by the gods, by the oracles and by anyone else who can claim the gift of prophecy. The theme is everywhere insisted upon. From the day that Aeneas set forth from ruined Troy, no power on earth or in heaven could deflect the Roman people from attaining their destined end. Now, with the triumph of Augustus, the old era of struggle and conquest has come to an end, and a new golden age is about to dawn. 'Venerable Faith and the Home, with Romulus and Remus, shall make the laws; the grim steel-welded gates of war shall be locked.' (*Aen.*, I, 290 f.)

Cicero had nothing to say about the operation of Fate in the fulfilment of Rome's destiny. If there was any supernatural agent at work, it was the will of the gods. The gods were open to prayer and they could be propitiated. Their favour was worth having, and the Roman state had rightly maintained a punctilious observance of the established religious rites. In Virgil, however, we find the view expressed that, though the interference of the gods in human affairs might be decisive in the short term, in the long run the ordinances of Fate must prevail. Thus Juno vents her hatred for the Trojans by raising storms, wars and other obstacles in their path; but, however difficult she may make their task, she cannot prevent their arrival in Latium or the founding of the city. In the end, even the mother of the gods must submit to the decree of Fate.

It remains to say a few words about the conception of the empire as we find it expressed in the literary remains of the Augustan period and after. The Romans, for Virgil, are 'lords of the world' (*rerum domini*) granted an 'empire without end' (*imperium sine fine*); and Ovid claimed that Jupiter, surveying the whole world from his seat on the Capitol, could see no land that was not under the rule of Rome.[39] Of course, Rome had boundaries beyond which warlike nations maintained a precarious independence. But such peoples lived on the border between Rome and the darkness of the unknown wasteland. They did not constitute a separate world. Since the fall of Carthage and the defeat of Macedon, Rome was the dominant power in the world; all other cities and nations, whatever degree of autonomy they might claim, existed only in their relationship to Rome. For the Roman citizen, an ordered and meaningful existence was possible only within the framework provided by laws, the customs and the institutions of the city. Outside the city, life lacked definition. Rome, like any other city-state, was the world in which men lived. It was a cosmos; and, already by the time of Cicero, this cosmos was increasingly identified with the natural order.[40]

This identification of Rome with the order of nature not only served to stress the permanence of the state. It also conveyed the impression that the present state of affairs was totally different from that which prevailed in the heroic days of the old republic. We see the difference most clearly in the historians. Livy is perhaps the last to see human affairs as a field in which great issues are at stake and fundamental changes take place. For Tacitus or for Ammianus Marcellinus, Rome has become the eternal city. Events no longer follow each other to form a coherent and purposeful development. History is the record of endless frontier wars, conspiracies and palace intrigues. But essentially nothing changes. The empire stands fast, as indestructible as the heavens above and the earth below.

In the later empire, the Christian apologist, Lactantius, could interpret his gruesome predictions of the coming apocalypse with the observation: 'It is obvious that the actual fall of things must come fairly soon, except that so long as Rome stands nothing of the sort need be feared. But when that head of the world has fallen, and the downward rush begins, as the sybil foretells, who would doubt that an end had come to human affairs and the world in general? It is the state that hitherto sustains everything.'[41] But, except to the devotees of an alien creed, the proposition that Rome could fall was unthinkable. Even when, in AD 415, Alaric and his Goths sacked the city and left it in ashes, Rome had not fallen. A few years after the disaster, Rutilius Namatianus found it not absurd to salute Rome as the city whose dominion coincides with the bounds of nature and whose achievement it is to have 'made a city of what was erstwhile a world'. Then, after invoking the memory of Aeneas and Romulus and recalling the various disasters the city had met with in bygone days, the poet observes that 'things which cannot be sunk rise again with greater energy, sped higher in their rebound from the lowest depths'. The city which survived the onslaughts of Samnite, Gaul and Carthaginian will also survive the Goth. 'Spread forth,' the poet sings, 'the laws that are to last throughout the ages of Rome; alone you need not dread the distaffs of the Fates.' The city has survived 1169 years, and 'the span which remains is subject to no bounds, so long as earth shall stand firm and heaven uphold the stars'.[42]

Chapter Four

Foundation and *eschatos*

I have suggested that a political myth is a set of similar arguments the individual meanings of which can not be determined apart from their context. Our discussion of the Roman Foundation Myth illustrates this point. Although far from comprehensive, it shows that, as the myth was transmitted from one generation to the next, its meaning and content changed giving us a series of individually distinct versions. None of these versions can be said to embody the 'true' meaning of the myth. Nor is there a single 'core' doctrine to which all versions, however diverse, can be reduced. Had we been able to discuss the later uses to which the myth was put—for instance, by opponents of papal power in the Middle Ages, by republican orators during the French Revolution or by Italian Fascists in the twentieth century—the point would have been made even clearer. A political myth is not a world-view which somehow persists unchanged through all its particular manifestations. It is, rather, what Wittgenstein would call a 'family' of arguments.

It is beyond the scope of this essay to attempt a complete classification of political myths; but we must, at least, make a broad distinction between foundation myths and eschatological myths. Of these two types, foundation myths are probably the more common. They are defined as a class by the fact that they explain the present in terms of a creative act that took place in the past. This act is sometimes sufficiently remote to be little more than a legend, but, in most cases, it is an actual and often quite recent historical event which has been dramatized for the purposes of political argument. The American Myth of the Founding Fathers and the Russian Myth of the October Revolution are, in this respect, more typical than the Roman Foundation Myth. There is, in principle, no limit to the ways in which such myths can be used, but they lend themselves especially to arguments justifying a *status quo*. They are conservative myths, even where the event mythologized happens to be a revolution—and herein they differ radically from eschatological myths.

Eschatological myths are myths concerned with 'the last things', the events with which the world as we know it comes to an end. The end of the world, the *eschatos*, is typically a cataclysmic act of destruction, a universal conflagration in which all things are reduced to the chaos from which they once emerged. 'This idea,' Bultmann tells us, 'is undoubtedly reached by conceiving the course of the world on the analogy of the annual periodicity of nature; as the seasons of the year follow each other, so do the corresponding periods in the course of the world, comprising the so-called "year of the world" or "the great world-year".'[1] Eliade also associates the great world-year with the eschatological traditions of the West. 'In proportion as the cosmic cycle became longer, the idea of the perfection of the beginning tended to imply a complementary idea: that, *for something genuinely new to begin, the vestiges and ruins of the old cycle must be completely destroyed*. In other words, to obtain an *absolute* beginning, the end of a World must be total.'[2]

In classical antiquity, certain cosmological doctrines did indeed embody notions of this kind. The Stoics, for instance, thought of the world-year as coming to an end, not perhaps when the world grows old and decrepit in the biological sense, but when all the permutations and combinations possible in the universe had been exhausted and, particularly, when all the heavenly bodies had returned to their exact original positions. At this point, they argued, the world would end and the whole process would start again from the beginning. 'Socrates and Plato will exist again and every man with his friends and his fellow citizens; he will suffer the same and do the same. Every city, every village and field will grow again. And this restoration will not happen once, but the same will return without limit and end.'[3]

The Stoic theory makes the point that, if a completely new beginning is to be made, nothing of the old must remain. There must be no possibility left unrealized. The old world must be used up or consumed *in toto*. But such a doctrine is speculative rather than mythical in character. It tells no story, and it leaves no room for human action. Moreover, its connection with eschatological myths is not as close as Bultmann and Eliade would have us believe. In myths, the end of the world is not always envisaged either as a return to the origins or as a new beginning. Indeed, many eschatological myths do not speak of the end of the world at all. Instead, they depict the *eschatos* as being the complete reversal of a certain state of affairs *within* the world. The old order is abolished and the new order comes into being, but the world as such remains. It is true that certain features of cosmological eschatologies appear in mythical arguments, but we cannot conclude from this that the latter were therefore derived from the former. No analogy, however striking, can stand as proof of a causal relationship.

The Christian Myth of the Millennium

We do not know precisely when eschatological myths began to circulate at Rome, but it is clear that, by the time of Augustus, such myths were both numerous and well established. The comet that appeared after the assassination of Julius Caesar was widely believed to be the herald of a new age; coins of the year 43 BC bear the symbols of power, fertility and the Golden Age; and the works of Virgil are replete with eschatological expectations.[4] These manifestations were harmless enough; but some of the doctrines that came from the East were not. Mysterious prophecies proclaimed the end of Rome and the transfer of power to Asia; and some held out the promise of a totally reconstructed society. 'A great fire or flood, the advent of a just monarch, or the descent of a bloodthirsty barbarian horde, would be the sign of the turning upside down of classes and values, a reversal of fortunes in favour of the oppressed.'[5] Suetonius reports that Augustus was sufficiently worried to collect and burn more than two thousand prophetic writings, 'retaining only the Sibylline books and making a choice even among those'. (*Aug.*, xxxi, 2.) However, the efforts of Augustus and his successors were to no avail. Eschatological doctrines continued to flourish and nowhere more so than among members of the growing Christian community.

The ancients had considered the world either as being forever the same or as repeating itself endlessly in identical cycles. For the Christian, however, the world was in no sense eternal. It had a beginning and it would have an end. The beginning was, as related in *Genesis*, the story of how God created the world followed by man's original sin and his expulsion from the Garden of Eden. The end was the tale of the final judgement in which the saved were to be separated from the damned and the world destroyed. Between these two points unfolded the great drama of man's career on earth, the climax of which was the coming of Christ to redeem fallen men and announce the kingdom to come. Christian doctrine, in other words, was founded on a dramatic narrative, a myth of great complexity and capable of infinite variation.

The view that the world is transitory, that it was created by God and will in the fullness of time be destroyed, carried with it two far-reaching implications. As the ancients saw it, time was cyclical and, in a world of flux, the only fixed point of reference for man was nature, the self-moving and self-sustaining cosmos. But, for the Christian, nature could no longer serve as a fixed point to which men might refer in the conduct of their lives. The fixed point now became God; and God, as Lactantius said, stood apart from the world he had created as the craftsman stands apart from his artefact.[6] In this sense, Christian practice was fundamentally other-worldly. The second implication was that time became linear and irreversible rather than cyclical. Both the beginning and the end were unique events. They had no precedent and they would not be repeated.

The doctrine of man's original sin and his fall from grace merely served to underline the other-worldly attitudes implied in the doctrine of creation. In the Garden of Eden, man had been in perfect harmony with God, with the world and with himself. As a result of his fall, this harmony was broken. Having lost his true home, he became a wanderer on the face of the earth, a tormented creature torn by the conflict between the flesh and spirit, between the forces of Satan and the hosts of the Heavenly City. His estrangement from the world was manifest, not only in that he now had to wrest a precarious living from the soil, but also in that he was a mortal and transient being. This was particularly significant. The Roman had, we recall, regarded his life as a citizen as being one with the life of his city. Death, in the sense of total extinction, was possible only through exclusion from public life or by the destruction of the city itself. The Christian, however, felt no such identity, either with the city in which he lived or with the natural order, the cosmopolis of which the Stoics asserted that all men were citizens. He was the total outcast whose lot was death unless he could establish a relationship with God in whom alone there was life. This relationship, however, required an abnegation or contempt of the self leading to a complete trust in God and obedience to his will. Here again, we note the difference between the Christian view and that which prevailed among the ancients. For all their controversies, the ancient moralists had agreed that man's end is to be attained here on earth and by his own efforts. But, for the Christian, not only was the true end of man to be achieved in a world infinitely remote from the one in which he now found himself, but sin had so corrupted human nature that man was rendered incapable of either knowing or attaining his ultimate end. Only his faith and the arbitrary grace of God could save him.

It appears that the earliest Christians regarded the end of the world, not as an event destined to take place in the future, but as one that was already occurring. They were themselves 'the community of the end-time, an eschatological phenomenon'.[7] The second coming and the final judgement lay close at hand. However, as time wore on and the expected *eschatos* failed to materialize, the Christians revised their views. Their eschatological hopes were not abandoned, but, as they became accustomed to waiting, the expected end of the world was removed into the indefinite future. Times of want and war, combined with sporadic acts of oppression, did, however, spark off visions of an imminent cosmic catastrophe, and a body of militant eschatological literature accumulated. Some of this survives in the writings of Commodianus, Irenaeus and, above all, in Book vii of Lactantius's *Divine Institutes*, an apologetic work probably composed in the early fourth century.

The world, Lactantius tells us, will last for only six thousand years, calculated from the day of creation. As these six thousand years draw to a close—and the time, Lactantius suggests, is near—the state of human affairs will deteriorate. 'All justice will be confounded, and the laws will be destroyed . . . there will be neither security, nor government, nor any rest from evils. For all the earth will be in a state of tumult; wars will everywhere rage; all nations will be in arms,' and 'the sword will traverse the world, mowing down everything, and laying low all things as a crop'. (*Div. Inst.*, vii, 15.) This wretched confusion will be heralded by the destruction of Rome and the transfer of power back to Asia: 'the East will again bear rule, and the West be reduced to servitude'. (ibid.)

The fall of Rome will be followed by a period of war and civil riot in the course of which ten kings will arise 'who will divide the world, not to govern but to consume it'. (*Div. Inst.*, vii, 16.) A conqueror will come from the North, destroy three of the kings in Asia and be recognized as overlord by the rest. His rule, however, will bring no relief to a war-torn world. The natural order itself will rebel and distintegrate. Floods, plagues and famine will become commonplace. The fruit will wither on the tree, the fountains will be dried up and the waters will be turned to blood. The very atmosphere will become corrupt and pestilential; 'the year will be shortened, and the month diminished, and the day contracted into a short space; and the stars shall fall in great numbers, so that all the heaven will appear dark without any lights. The loftiest mountains also will fall, and be levelled with the plains; the sea will be rendered unnavigable.' (ibid.)

At this point, a trumpet will sound from heaven and men, quaking with fear, will call upon God; but he will not hear them. Anxiety will render the nights sleepless and death welcome. Then, as the end draws near, a prophet will be sent to turn men to the knowledge of God. But a great king, the Antichrist, will come from the East and, having killed the prophet, will call himself God and men will worship him. The few surviving righteous will flee into solitary places. When the Antichrist hears of this, he will gather his army and surround the righteous on the mountain where they have taken refuge. They will call upon God and, at this point, Christ, the Judge and Avenger, will descend with a company of angels to the middle of the earth 'and there shall go before Him an unquenchable fire, and the power of the angels shall deliver into the hands of the just that multitude which has surrounded the mountain, and they shall be slain from the third hour until the evening, and blood shall flow like a torrent; and all his forces being destroyed, the wicked one shall alone escape, and his power shall perish from him'. (*Div. Inst.*, vii, 19.) The Antichrist will renew the war, but, in the fourth battle, he will suffer a decisive defeat. Together with all the other princes who have harassed the world, he will be led in chains to the victor who will condemn them all to the tortures they richly deserve. Then, at last, the lower regions will be opened and those of the dead who had 'been exercised in the religion of God' will rise to be judged according to their merits. But those, who, while still alive, remained unacquainted with the Almighty will stay in their pits 'since the Holy Scriptures testify that the wicked shall not arise to judgement'. (*Div. Inst.*, vii, 20.)

After the judgement, the Millennium will commence. The righteous will multiply, and a sacred city will be planted in the middle of the earth. Here God will dwell together with his people. The darkness will be taken away from the world; the moon will become as bright as the sun, and the sun will be seven times brighter than it is now. 'And the earth will open its fruitfulness, and bring forth most abundant fruits of its own accord; the rocky mountains shall drop with honey; streams of wine shall run down, and rivers flow with milk.' (*Div. Inst.*, vii, 24.) The world will rejoice and all nature exult, 'being rescued and set free from the dominion of evil and impiety, and guilt and error'. (ibid.) All will be peace and tranquillity. 'Lions and calves shall stand together at the manger, the wolf shall not carry off the sheep, the hound shall not hunt for prey; hawks and eagles shall not injure; the infant shall play with serpents.' (ibid.)

At the end of the thousand years, Satan will be let loose from his prison and 'will assemble all the nations, which shall then be under the dominion of the righteous, that they may make war against the holy city', (*Div. Inst.*, vii, 26) and the city will be besieged by a vast host. But then, 'the last anger of God shall come upon the nations'. For three days, the sun will stand still and the earth will blaze with fire, during which time the people of God will be concealed in caves while the nations of the earth are consumed. When this is done, 'the world shall be renewed by God, and the heavens shall be folded together, and the earth shall be changed, and God shall transform men into the similitude of angels, and they shall be white as snow; and they shall always be employed in the sight of the Almighty, and shall make offerings to their Lord and serve

Him for ever'. (*Div. Inst.*, vii, 26.) At the same time, a second resurrection will take place, 'in which the unrighteous shall be raised to everlasting punishments' and 'shall be burnt for ever with perpetual fire in the sight of angels and the righteous'. (ibid.)

The *eschatos*, as Lactantius pictures it, has many features that suggest a purely natural process. Indeed, he cites with approval prophecies describing the end-time as 'the last old age of the wearied and wasting world'. (*Div. Inst.*, vii, 14.) But this physical decay and death of the world would be a disaster of no moral significance were it not that it provides the occasion for God's intervention in the affairs of men and for men's direct participation in this act of intervention. Although the remnant of the righteous besieged on the mountain are powerless to save themselves, they do not stand idly by when Christ the King descends to their rescue. It is into the hands of the righteous that the hordes of Antichrist are delivered, and it is they who shed the torrent of blood on which Lactantius dwells with such relish. The righteous are not themselves responsible for their predicament; neither do they owe their victory to their own efforts and abilities. The course of the drama is predetermined; but, within its framework, they have a part to play, and their merit lies in knowing their role and in the quality of their performance.

The Roman Foundation Myth was pre-eminently a political myth. It told the story of how a political society was founded, and it expressed the values and aspirations of those who benefited from the continued existence of that society. Lactantius, however, speaks for people who stand outside the political order and look upon it with distaste. He acknowledges that life under the empire is preferable to the state of affairs which will ensue when Rome falls; but, he tells us, 'the Sibyls openly say that Rome is doomed to perish, and that indeed by the judgement of God, because it held His name in hatred; and being the enemy of righteousness, it destroyed the people who kept the truth'. (*Div. Inst.*, vii, 15.) For all its merits, the empire is an abomination, and its fall is a necessary prelude to the victory of the righteous, a victory which will inaugurate a world in which politics is abolished.[8] The suggestion that the abolition of politics was something the empire had already achieved would have seemed a pointless quibble. For Lactantius, the empire is, in all relevant respects, the continuation of the old republic; and both are equally vicious, for as he says, there can be no justice or piety in any society that worships false gods. (*Div. Inst.*, v, 8.) His only comment on the political life, properly understood, is to reject as futile Cicero's hope for the immortality that glory might bring. (*Div. Inst.*, v, 19.)

By the time of St Augustine, when the Church had become well established, fulminations against the powers that be had ceased to be as pertinent as they were before. A determined effort was therefore made to halt the spread of eschatological ideas. Augustine himself argued that the Book of Revelation should be read as a spiritual allegory and that the Kingdom of Christ on earth was already actualized in the Catholic Church. His views were received as orthodox; millennialist beliefs were condemned as heretical; and the works of Irenaeus were expurgated. In place of membership in the community of the righteous, the faithful were invited to seek an individual salvation through the sacraments of the Church.[9] However, prophecies of the kingdom to come continued to circulate among the common people; and, time and time again, manifestations of popular unrest were accompanied by the preaching of eschatological doctrines.

National revolutionary myths

Norman Cohn describes the millennialist myths of the Middle Ages as 'revolutionary' myths. We know what he means, and it is perhaps pedantic to quibble, but the trouble with this use of the term is its implication that the medieval millennialists intended to bring about what we nowadays understand by a revolution. The medieval millennialists were certainly dangerous rebels; and, from time to time, they posed a serious threat to peace and security. But neither their deeds nor their myths were, in any strict sense, revolutionary. A revolution involves, among other things, an attack upon the state; and, since states are a relatively recent development, so are revolutions. If we are to look for revolutionary myths, we must turn to the polemical literature of those civil wars that troubled the birth of the modern nation-state.

Let us begin with France. In the early sixteenth century, the attempts of Francis I to consolidate the power of the monarchy provoked a debate as to the nature and limits of royal authority. Important conflicts of interest were involved. But the debate, though sometimes heated, was conducted entirely in the technical language of the civil lawyers. It was not until the outbreak of civil war (in 1562) that the issue became one of urgent popular concern and the arguments acquired an edge they had hitherto lacked. At first, the Huguenot rebels had justified their recourse to arms by claiming to defend the authority of the king against the usurpation of the House of Guise. But, when this claim ceased to be plausible, they fell back on the suggestion that they were fighting to recover the ancient laws and liberties of France. In his *Franco-Gallia*, published shortly after the Massacre of St Bartholomew (1571), Hotman raised this suggestion to the level of a full-blown mythical argument.

He opens by declaring that, only if the French return to their ancestral constitution can they hope to save their country from disaster.[10] This ancestral constitution was, he says, established in all its essentials by the ancient Gauls. Gaul was originally divided into a number of *civitates* all of which were elective monarchies in which royal authority was circumscribed by law, and the kings were no less accountable to their subjects than their subjects were to them. With the Roman conquest, the Gauls lost their ancient liberty; but they maintained their resistance to Roman domination, and, in their struggle, they called upon the aid of mercenaries from across the Rhine. These mercenaries were the Franks. Like the Gauls, the Franks were accustomed to a monarchical constitution, a constitution which in no way diminished the freedom they prized so highly. 'To obey a king,' Hotman observes, 'is not servitude; neither are all who are governed by kings for that reason to be counted as slaves but only such as submit themselves to the unbounded will of a tyrant, thief and executioner, as sheep resign themselves to the butcher's knife.'[11] The Franks drove out the Roman oppressors and combined with the Gauls to establish a united kingdom, Childeric being the first monarch elected by the joint suffrages of both peoples.

Hotman was, of course, aware of the argument that, according to Salic Law, the kingship of the Franks was hereditary. To this he replies that the laws of the Salian Franks in Germany did not apply in the kingdom of France and that, in any case, both the Salian Franks and the Franco-Gauls regarded the law of primogeniture as pertaining only to matters of private right. Whatever the Salian Franks might have done, the French had the right to elect and depose their kings. The constitution they established was, in fact, mixed in the manner recommended by the classical philosophers. Each year the king summoned a general assembly composed of the princes and magistrates of the realm together with representatives of the towns and provinces, and it was in these assemblies that all the business of the commonwealth was transacted. Not only did this arrangement serve as a check on powerful ministers of state, it also ensured that decisions were properly deliberated and, above all, that the liberty of the people was preserved; for, says Hotman, 'it is an essential part of liberty that those at whose cost and peril a thing is done should have it done by their authority and advice, for what concerns all should be approved by all'.[12] Such, then, was the ancient constitution which, Hotman claimed, was the birth-right of every natural Frenchman.

Allen remarks that, even by the standards of his time, Hotman's work is a poor piece of history, full of 'inaccuracies, confusions and misunderstandings'.[13] So, indeed, it is. But then Hotman did not intend to make a contribution to historical scholarship. He intended to vindicate the rights of his embattled co-religionists and to undermine the authority of what he regarded as a brutally oppressive government. It is true that he nowhere discusses contemporary events or developments, but the account he gives of the past carries implications which his public could hardly fail to notice.

The most obvious implication is that, in France, sovereign authority resides in the people acting through the Estates General and that this authority has recently been usurped by the crown. The present government is, therefore, unconstitutional; and the Huguenots are not rebels but patriotic citizens attempting to recover their constitutional rights. However, to this somewhat academic point Hotman adds an ambiguous but effective appeal to national sentiment. The French, he suggests, are Franco-Gauls, and their hereditary enemy is Rome. Though the legions have long since been expelled, Rome herself lives on; if the French today suffer from tyrannous government and civil disorder, they need only look to the turbulent origins of their nation to discover the reason why. For is not the hand of the ancient enemy discernible in the growing acceptance of Roman law? in the machinations of the queen mother, Catherine de' Medici? and, above all, in the policies and principles of the Catholic Church? Wherever the French are oppressed, the baleful influence of Rome is apparent. Indeed, the established order is not merely a departure from the traditional practices of the French people; it is an instrument of oppression wielded by an alien and hostile power. The Huguenot cause is, in short, identical with the cause of France. We can even detect a suggestion that, just as the Gauls were justified in summoning the Franks to their aid, so the Huguenots are entitled to accept the men and money from the Protestant states across the Rhine.

While Hotman and the Huguenots invoked the ancient glories of the Franco-Gauls to justify their stand against the crown, the somewhat similar Myth of the Norman Yoke was taking shape in England. Briefly, the main points of the myth are these. The early Anglo-Saxon inhabitants of England enjoyed a constitution in which the government was conducted through representative institutions and the liberty of all citizens was secured by the law. The Norman Conquest abolished this state of affairs and replaced it with the tyranny of an alien ruling class. The English, however, did not resign themselves to their lot but, with varying success, continued the struggle to recover the rights they had lost.

There were, as Christopher Hill points out, several versions of this doctrine current in the seventeenth century.[14] It appears, for instance, in the writings and pronouncements of the early Parliamentarian opposition to royal power. Men such as Coke and Pym found that appeals to the precedent of the ancient Anglo-Saxon constitution gave weight to their protest against arbitrary government and the enforcement of feudal dues. Generally speaking, the Parliamentarians took the view that the Norman Conquest, though drastic in its consequences, nevertheless left many authentic English institutions intact. The common law and trial by jury were cited as examples, and so, of course, was Parliament itself.[15]

The outbreak of the civil wars, however, engendered a more radical version of the myth. Cromwell's Ironsides saw themselves as enacting the last episode in the long saga of the English people. They felt, as Brailsford remarks, 'that on Marston Moor and Naseby Field they recovered what was lost at Hastings'.[16] A wave of anti-Norman feeling swept the ranks. The English were to have their ancient rights restored in full, and all relics of Norman oppression were to be rooted out. But the reforms envisaged by the soldiers and the Leveller pamphleteers who gave them their lead were far more extensive than anything Parliament was prepared to allow. The king, as William the Bastard's successor, was to be deposed; the House of Lords was to be abolished, for what were the lords but William the Conqueror's colonels? Every commoner was to have an equal voice in electing members to Parliament. And much else of the sort.[17]

Where the Levellers in the army pressed the case for the restoration of political rights, the Levellers in the countryside carried the implications of the myth one step further. To their minds, the destruction of Norman hegemony meant that the rights of the English to the 'land of their nativity' could be reasserted against the lords of the manor. They demanded, as one group put it, that 'all base Tenures by Copies, Oaths of Fealty, Homage, Fines at the will of the lord etc. (being the Conqueror's marks upon the people) may be taken away'.[18] Copyhold in particular came under attack as a Norman imposition and a 'badge of slavery', and freeholders were branded as the successors of William the Conqueror's soldiers.

It was thus that, in the late 1640s, the simplest and most uncompromising version of the myth took shape. As the Diggers on St George's Hill declared in their *Appeal to the House of Commons*: 'When William the Conqueror came in, he took the land from the English, both the Enclosures from the Gentry, and the Commons and waste land from the common people, and gave our land to his Norman soldiers.' Under Charles I, they reminded the House, the tyranny became so oppressive that 'you and we cried for a Parliament, and a Parliament was called, and wars, you know, presently begun, between the King, that represented William the Conqueror, and the body of the English people that were enslaved'. Parliament called upon the people to provide money and men and promised, in return, 'to make us a free people'. A covenant was made to this effect, 'you and we joyned purse and person together in this common cause', the Conqueror's successor was defeated in battle, 'and thereby we have recovered our selves from under that Norman yoak'. Now it rested with Parliament to make good its pledge; and for the Diggers this meant letting 'the common people have their Commons and waste lands set free to them, from all Norman enslaving Lords of Mannors'.[19] The Diggers did indeed ask that 'the Gentry have their inclosures free from all Norman enslaving intanglements whatsoever', but when they went on to denounce all landlords and freeholders as the heirs of William's army, Parliament could well be excused for thinking that there would be little room for the gentry in a Digger England. The Diggers were suppressed and eventually silenced.

The Myth of the Franco-Gauls and the Myth of the Norman Yoke are 'national revolutionary' myths in that they consist of appeals to the 'nation' against the arbitrary power of the state. In both cases, the nation is conceived as a 'people' which once possessed a political society but subsequently lost it and is now groaning under the yoke of an alien tyranny. And the upheavals, in the context of which these myths were formed, are represented, not as civil wars, but as attempts on the part of the people to expel a foreign invader. There is, of course, a significant difference. For Hotman, the French are a single nation composed of two peoples united in a common defiance of everything Roman; and the Romans are not so much an identifiable group within the population as enemies who do their destructive work from without. The Myth of the Norman Yoke, by contrast, depicts the population of England as divided into two mutually hostile peoples, one of which is alien to the soil on which it has planted itself. There is, in other words, no external enemy. The enemy is within, and he can be accurately identified by his political allegiance or (as the case may be) by his socio-economic status. But, despite this difference between the two myths, they share the general argument that, only when the land is purged of the foreigner and all his works, can the people become free and the state be transformed into a national state.

In their promise of a more perfect world to come, these myths recall the militant eschatologies of the Christian Church. But the similarity is no more than superficial. So far from rejecting *in toto* the temporal world, the revolutionaries of the sixteenth and seventeenth centuries incorporated into their vision of the world to come elements of what they took to be the real achievements of their historical ancestors. The revolution they envisaged entailed no cosmic catastrophe; it required no supernatural intervention; and it depended on the advent of no leader, prophet or messiah. Above all, it promised, not the abolition of politics, but the restoration of an authentic political society.

The Myth of the Aryan Race

The doctrines we have just discussed are sometimes cited as early examples of race-thinking. This is a mistake, but it is one that is easily made, for, though these doctrines contain nothing we can call an appeal to race, they bear an undoubted resemblance to certain later doctrines which do. Race-thinking, properly so called, entails the notion that a specific group of people, defined in terms of their common descent, possess genetically transmitted virtues which mark them off as being superior to the rest of humanity. Not surprisingly, this notion first took hold in the ranks of the hereditary nobility; and the man chiefly responsible for its introduction was the Comte de Boulainvilliers.

By the beginning of the eighteenth century, the French nobility had become acutely aware of their deteriorating political position. As many saw it, the cause of the decline was the fact that the monarchy, bent on achieving despotic power, had systematically encouraged and promoted to high office ambitious members of the Third Estate. Boulainvilliers himself doubted whether the damage could now be undone, but he felt that, at least, a stand should be made. Every historical state of note, he maintained, has been ruled by an aristocracy composed of men who owe their position solely to their noble blood. Such was the government of Rome in her heyday; and such was the system the Frankish invaders established in Gaul. The Franks were indeed (as Hotman described them) a freedom-loving people who elected their kings and governed themselves through popular assemblies; but (contrary to Hotman) they did not combine with the natives to found a united kingdom but, rather, reduced them to subjection and set themselves up as a hereditary caste of soldiers and magistrates. The land was theirs by right of conquest, and whatever property the Gauls were allowed to retain was burdened with tribute. The Franks themselves remained exempt from all obligations except that of bearing arms; and they held their individual lands and offices in trust, not to the king (who was no more than *primus inter pares*), but to the nation as a whole.[20]

This, then, was the origin of the distinction between *la noblesse* and *la roture*. It is not always clear what significance Boulainvilliers attaches to blood and descent in the maintenance of this distinction. In one place, he suggests that intermarriage between Franks and Gauls was not as serious a deviation from the established constitution as the admission of Gauls to the army.[21] But elsewhere he deplores the fact that nobles of reduced circumstances 'no longer scruple to mix their blood with that of the vilest commoner', and he concludes by castigating the king for failing to maintain the difference between the orders, 'as if, indeed, his grandeur depended on promoting an ill-regulated confusion of blood in all his subjects, like that established among the Turks'.[22]

But, if Boulainvilliers was ambivalent, his disciples were not. In the aristocratic ethic of the late eighteenth century, pure descent in a free-born stock was the *sine qua non* for rightful access to high office. By the time of the French Revolution, this doctrine had become sufficiently influential to provoke a series of impassioned replies. Babeuf inveighed against the supposed right of conquest; and Sieyes recommended that the Third Estate 'repatriate to the Franconian forests all the families who wildly claim to descend from the race of the conquerors'.[23] But, during the Revolution itself, the strictly racial aspects of Boulain-villiers's doctrine received, if anything, an even sharper emphasis. Many of the nobles who fled to England and Germany found that they had more in common with their aristocratic hosts than they had with their fellow-countrymen. Increasingly, they came to regard themselves as members of an international caste bound together by common descent; and, in the thinking of men such as Dubuat-Nancay and Montlosier, the Revolution was conceived as a revolt of the Gallo-Roman rabble which it was the duty of the Germanic aristocracy of Europe to suppress.[24]

It is, as Hannah Arendt remarks, curious that, from these early times, French racial theorists 'have supported the Germanism or at least the superiority of the Nordic peoples as against their own countrymen'. Not even the rise of German nationalism, directed as it was against the French, could change the course of racial myth-making in France.[25] This may be so. However, there were other developments which did change the course of racial myth-making, not only in France, but in

Germany as well; and the first of these was the 'discovery' of the Aryan race.

In 1788, Sir William Jones had advanced the thesis that several European languages belonged to the same linguistic group as Sanskrit and must, therefore, have had the same origin. It was an easy step to conclude that, if there was an original language, there must have been an original people which spoke this language, and that this people was the ancestor of all the Indo-European or (as some would have it) Indo-Germanic nations. Distinguished philologists, such as Jacob Grimm and Franz Bopp, refined the linguistic aspects of the theory; but it was left to Gobineau to combine it with traditional aristocratic race-thinking and present the synthesis as a total explanation of human history. His *Essay on the Inequality of the Human Races* (1853) had a single simple theme: 'that all civilizations derive from the white race, that none can exist without its help, and that a society is great and brilliant only so far as it preserves the blood of the noble group that created it'.[26] Through conquest and migration, he suggests, the Aryans founded all the mighty empires known to history; but, in every case, they ended by mixing their blood with that of their racially inferior subjects, and thus they lost those intrinsic qualities on which their greatness was based. The civilizations they had created kept their momentum for a while, but, since the impulse which sustained their vitality was gone, they eventually collapsed. And this, according to Gobineau, is why societies degenerate; 'the *degenerate* man properly so called, is a different being, from the racial point of view, from the heroes of the great ages'.[27]

Gobineau himself believed that the mingling of races had now been carried so far that mankind was doomed to final obliteration. But other theorists were less pessimistic. In 1859, Max Müller delighted London society with his descriptions of how the adventurous Aryans spread their conquests from the Ganges to the Loire; and, in the same year, Adolphe Pictet presented the Aryans as a race 'destined by Providence some day to dominate the entire globe'.[28] Müller later repudiated his facile identification of linguistic communities with racial groups; but the idea of the Aryan race was, by then, too firmly fixed to be eradicated. Indeed, by the turn of the century, it had become the stock-in-trade of racial myth-makers in almost every country of Northern Europe.

Another formative influence on the political myth-makers of the nineteenth century was Darwin's theory of evolution. This theory was, of course, scientific rather than practical in character, but, because it entailed a general view of nature, it was easily adapted to serve the purposes of practical argument. In fact, political moralists of every persuasion found in Darwin an apparently scientific vindication of their preconceived points of view. Spencer, for instance, cited the laws of natural selection to support his advocacy of a competitive society; Kropotkin, with equal facility, argued that the struggle for existence favours those species in which the instinct for co-operation is most fully developed.[29] But nowhere was the theory more eagerly seized upon than among the proponents of racial supremacy. Since the time of Boulain-villiers, race-thinkers had been embarrassed by the suggestion that the right of conquest is contrary to natural law. But now the Darwinian view that nature achieves her purpose by destroying the weak and preserving the strong provided a ready answer. Moreover, the theory could be used to account for the differentiation of the human species into a number of unequally gifted races; and it even lent weight to the view that the salvation of mankind depended on the ultimate victory and predominance of its noblest part. Darwinism, in short, supplied the racial myth-makers with a concept of nature and a theoretical framework which enabled them to reconcile their political claims with the latest scientific fashions.

The last major ingredient that helped shape the Myth of the Aryan Race was anti-Semitism. The history of this famous prejudice goes back to the Middle Ages, but the characteristic role of the Jew as the polar opposite and hereditary enemy of the Aryan was not developed until the latter part of the nineteenth century.[30] This is not altogether surprising. For so long as race-thinking retained its association with the aristocratic cause, the eternal antagonist, which the dramatic logic of a political myth requires, had to be the revolutionary rabble of France, the despised Gallo-Roman plebs. But, with the unification of Germany and the subsequent sharpening of national enmities in Europe, the aristocratic overtones of Aryan supremacy were gradually submerged (though not entirely forgotten), and the notion of race was uneasily associated with that of the nation. To be a Frenchman or a German was, in the view of many patriots, to be an Aryan; and the danger to the nation lay, not with the restless urban proletariat, but with the insidious alien who exploited their labour and corrupted their minds with anti-national ideas. In the work of Eduard Drumont and his like, this alien was revealed as the Jew. The Aryan, Drumont declares, has always been at odds with the Semite. Time and again, the Semite attempted to reduce the Aryan by force of arms, only to suffer defeat; but now he believes his victory is certain. 'It is no longer the Carthaginian or the Saracen, who is in the vanguard, it is the Jew—he has replaced violence with cunning. Dangerous invasion has given way to silent, progressive and slow encroachment. The noisy armed hordes have been replaced by single individuals, gradually forming little groups, advancing sporadically, unobtrusively occupying all the jobs, from the lowest to the highest in the land.'[31] This historical scenario, together with the conception of the Jew as a materialistic and culture-destroying parasite, was to be endlessly embellished in the controversies surrounding the Dreyfus affair. It then became the major theme of Houston Stewart Chamberlain's monumental *The Foundations of the Nineteenth Century*. And, finally, it was adopted in all its essentials by the propagandists of the National Socialist movement.

The conditions in which National Socialism achieved its success are too well known to require much comment. The First World War had caused a massive dislocation of public and private life; and the hope that peace would bring stability was, for many Germans, dashed by the period of inflation, unemployment and civil unrest that followed. In patriotic circles, it became common form to insist that Germany had lost the war, not through military defeat, but through an act of political betrayal, and that most of the ills from which the country suffered could be traced to the peace terms imposed at Versailles. The fact that the Weimar government had accepted these terms, coupled with its manifest inability to solve the continuing economic crisis, brought the values and procedures of liberal democracy increasingly into contempt. Dissatisfaction was particularly rife among the returning soldiers, many of whom were unable to adjust to civilian life and recalled with affection the comradeship of the trenches and the sense of national purpose achieved by total mobilization. All this contributed to a growing disenchantment with the established political order and to a mounting demand for drastic remedies. And it was in response to this demand that Hitler invoked the Myth of the Aryan Race.

Hitler's version of the myth does not differ substantially from those propounded by his nineteenth-century predecessors. He insists, as they do, that 'struggle is the father of all things' and that 'virtue lies in blood'.[32] If, he argues, two beings of different races are allowed to cross, the offspring will stand higher than the racially lower parent, but not as high as the higher one, and will therefore succumb in the struggle for existence. 'Such mating,' he adds, 'is contrary to the will of Nature for a higher breeding of all life.'[33] It is this crudely Darwinian view that gives his account of the past its prescriptive force. The Aryan, he asserts, is the sole creator of cultures, 'the Prometheus of mankind from whose bright forehead the divine spark of genius has sprung at all times, forever kindling anew that fire of knowledge which illumined the night of silent mysteries and thus caused man to climb the path to mastery over the other beings of this earth'.[34] The definitive characteristic of the Aryan is his idealism, that is, his innate ability to subordinate his individual interests to the common good; and if 'the Jew possesses no culture-creating force', this is because 'idealism, without which there is no true higher development of man, is not present in him and never was present'.[35] Indeed, the whole history of man can be seen as a conflict between Aryan idealism and Jewish materialism. And always it has been the failure of the Aryan to maintain the purity of his stock that has caused his downfall. His magnificent achievements were blighted and his empires fell because he transgressed against the principle of blood purity; he mixed with his racially inferior subjects and thus brought upon himself the fate which eventually overtook him, 'for the fall of man in paradise has always been followed by his expulsion'.[36]

One of the peculiarities of the National Socialist myth-makers is their awareness of the fact that they are making myths. 'The inner voice now demands,' said Alfred Rosenberg, 'that the myth of blood and the myth of soul, race and ego, *Volk* and personality, blood and honour; that this myth, alone and uncompromisingly, must penetrate, bear and determine all life.'[37] Of course, they did not use the term 'myth' in any pejorative sense; they used it in something like Chamberlain's sense of 'a metaphysical view of the world *sub specie oculorum*'.[38] But they were in no doubt that myth, as a mode of discourse, is the expression of a practical purpose; and their very consciousness of what they were doing enabled them to reinterpret and absorb the myths of other ages. Hitler's explicit identification of original sin with racial mixing is a case in point. It is an identification to which Hitler constantly returns; and it illustrates, in a remarkable way, the manner in which one myth can be made to appropriate the content of another and thus facilitate the process of conversion. So far from being contrary to Christian doctrine, the Myth of the Aryan Race could be read as having revealed its deeper meaning; and pious Germans could become National Socialists without abandoning their religious faith.

The other major myth which the National Socialists invoked was the old Germanic tale of *ragnarök*. This myth, which described the death of the gods in a final combat with the forces of evil, seemed to confirm the gloomy forecasts of Gobineau. The National Socialists, however, took a more optimistic view. Though the mighty empires established by the original Aryans had passed away, uncorrupted remnants of the race still survived, especially among the German people. Recalling their ancient valour, this people had recently engaged in a desperate struggle to maintain their national existence, but, at the very moment of their victory, they were stabbed in the back by the Jew in their midst. This was their *ragnarök*, 'when dark satanic strengths became active behind the victorious armies of 1914; when once again there dawned an age when the Fenris Wolf broke his chains, when Hell, exuding the odour of decay, moved over the earth and the *Midgardschlange* stirred the oceans of the world'.[39] But the German people, though defeated, were not destroyed. Indeed, alerted by their recent disaster to the magnitude of their danger and inspired by a renewed awareness of their racial destiny, they would rise again; they would purge their ranks of all non-Aryan elements and implement a policy of national regeneration based on the principle of racial purity. This done, Aryan armies would once more traverse the world bearing the gifts of a higher culture to the teeming masses of inferior races. Thus *ragnarök* was simultaneously invoked and transcended—*aufgehoben*, as Hegel would doubtlessly have put it.

The Myth of the Aryan Race (in its National Socialist version) is similar to the national revolutionary myths of an earlier age in that it makes an appeal to the 'nation' against the state. However, there are two significant differences. Firstly, the National Socialists carried their hostility to the Weimar Republic to the point of calling for a complete abolition of politics. The Third Reich, the state of the Aryan race, was not to be a constituted political order deriving its authority from the law; it was to be the instrument for the achievement of a racial destiny, and its authority was to rest on a mystical communion between the leader and his people. Hitler himself emphasized the point. The leader, he said, is the extraordinary man who has a clear insight into the needs of his time and who, by some uncanny instinct, points the way to their fulfilment and inspires general confidence that he, and he alone, is the man to carry out the task which history at that moment requires. And Carl Schmitt, a distinguished law professor, gave the vital gloss—he argued that the Third Reich, though legally constituted, derived its real legitimacy from 'the continuous and truthful contact between leader and followers', which, in turn, depended on 'an unconditional similarity of racial stock'.[40] Whatever else it was to be, the state of the Aryan race was not to be a political society.

Secondly, the National Socialist myth suffered from an ambiguity which (as we have noted) was inherent in race-thinking from the outset. The notion of race never completely lost the anti-national connotations it had acquired at the time of its origin. And, though Hitler sometimes spoke as if he regarded the whole German nation as composed of undiluted Aryan stock, it is clear that this was not his real view. 'The conception of the nation,' he remarked in conversation, 'has become meaningless. We have to get rid of this false conception and set in its place the conception of race. The New Order cannot be conceived in terms of the national boundaries of the peoples with a historic past, but in terms of race that transcend these boundaries.' And his plans for the ss were that it should be an élite drawn from the Aryan elements of all nationalities. 'The active sections in nations, the militant, the Nordic sections, will rise again and become the ruling element over these shop-keepers and pacifists, these puritans and speculators and busybodies. . . . There will not be much left then of the cliches of nationalism, and precious little among us Germans. Instead, there will be an understanding between the various language elements of the one good ruling race.'[41]

The demand for a morally coherent world

I have argued that the Roman Foundation Myth discloses a desire to achieve a morally coherent world. The millennialist myths of the early Christian Church and the revolutionary myths of our own time display, I suggest, the same concern—though not, of course in the same way. Where the Roman citizen looked to the old republic, the Christian millennialist looked to the Kingdom of Christ and the Leveller looked to a free commonwealth in which the perfection of the old Anglo-Saxon constitution would be restored. But despite the differences in formulation, the practical preoccupation at work is the same.

By a morally coherent world, I mean a just world, i.e. one in which merit invariably receives its reward. Hesiod describes such a world in his *Works and Days* (225–50). Men who are righteous, he says, always flourish. 'Peace, the nurse of children, is abroad in their land, and all-seeing Zeus never decrees cruel war against them. Neither famine nor disaster ever haunt men who do true justice. . . .' But, he adds, where cruelty and violence prevail, 'the son of Cronos lays great trouble upon the people, famine and plague together, so that the men perish away, and their women do not bear children, and their houses become few'. The salient feature of Hesiod's account is the suggestion that the future can be predicted on the basis of purely moral considerations. If we wish to know, for instance, whether a woman will bear children or whether the harvest will be successful, the factors a physician or meteorologist might adduce are beside the point. The relevant question is whether the people concerned are just and therefore deserve to prosper. Similarly, Thucydides tells us, the citizens of Melos felt sure they would beat the Athenians, despite the inferiority of their forces, 'because,' as they said, 'we are righteous, and you against whom we contend are unrighteous'. (*Pel. Wars.*, v, 104.)

The confident assertion that we already live in a morally coherent world is a common theme in Western literature, but it is nowhere near as common as the complaint that we do not. The Roman poets, we recall, never tired of commenting on the discrepancy between what virtue deserves and fortune brings. Though the ancients hoped that hard work and foresight might establish a rough correlation between merit and reward, they knew that this correlation was one which any sudden mischance might upset. The wrath which this state of affairs often provoked was, of course, unreasonable. As Seneca said: 'They are mad who lay to the charge of the gods the cruelty of the sea, excessive rains, and the stubbornness of winter. . . . It is not because of us that the universe brings back winter and summer; these have their own laws by which the divine plan operates. We have too high a regard for ourselves if we deem ourselves worthy to be the cause of such mighty movements.' (*De Ira*, II, xxvii, 2.) But, with the best will in the world, few men were able to maintain a studied indifference in the face of unwarranted misfortune. Stoic detachment might well have appealed to those whose economic position isolated them from the more serious consequences of nature's operations. But, for the peasant who lived by his work, unseasonable weather was more than a transient inconvenience. It was a disaster the injustice of which was in no way diminished by his sense of impotence. He had needs the satisfaction of which could not be postponed indefinitely if he was to continue to live. He had to feed and clothe himself, and he had to do so in a world that was indifferent to his welfare and governed by forces beyond his control. From this predicament, there was no escape. He lacked the freedom which only wealth could bring; and it was the fact that his life was thus governed by necessity that exposed him to the tyranny of fortune.

There was another point of which the ancients were keenly aware. In attempting to survive, men are often compelled to act in a way which they do not prescribe themselves. In a sense, their deeds are not their own. They behave, not as moral individuals pursuing their chosen ends, but as the functioning parts of a greater whole or as the agents of an enterprise governed by some larger purpose. For this reason, Aristotle argued that no man compelled to labour for his subsistence could live the good life, that is, a life guided by moral reason. It was not that labourers and artisans were inherently incapable of virtue. The point was that considerations of moral right and wrong could come into play only when a man's more pressing material needs were met. Necessity, as the adage had it, knows no law; and he whose needs and circumstances make him subject to necessity cannot be, in any proper sense, a moral being.[42]

The contemporaries of Hesiod lived in a world that was only to an insignificant degree political or social. Outside the city, bounded by its walls, lay the vast and ultimately chaotic realm of nature. Ambitious men with a penchant for violence posed a constant threat to the maintenance of justice within the city, but it was the vagaries of wind and weather rather than the whims of tyrants that chiefly oppressed and exasperated the common folk. The chosen few sought refuge in a political life which, because it was ordered by law, provided a modicum of justice; the rest either trusted their luck or pinned their hopes on doctrines which promised a revolution in the only place where it mattered, namely, in the order of nature as a whole.

The contemporaries of Marx, however, were entering a different world: the modern industrial society. The changes of the seasons which governed the life of Hesiod's farmer were here of little or no significance. Their place was taken by the movements of the economic system. The world was no longer a natural world which men shared with the gods; it was a social world which men themselves had constructed and which they shared with no one but their fellow men. But, as Marx was one of the first to remark, the conquest of nature had not achieved the liberation of man. The political economists might discover the laws of the market place and declare them to be working for the general good, but the individual worker found that neither his labour nor its product were his to command. They belonged to a world of commodities which operated according to laws of its own, and the worker himself was 'consequently exposed to all the vicissitudes of competition, to all the fluctuations of the market'.[43] Trade recessions and unemployment struck in the same arbitrary fashion as droughts, floods and storms at sea.

Like his ancient counterpart, the modern worker found himself in a predicament which, not only made him the victim of injustice, but also compelled him to act contrary to his better nature. In Marx's view, this predicament had its root in the social division of labour. 'For,' he said, 'as soon as the distribution of labour comes into being, each man has a particular, exclusive sphere of activity, which is forced upon him and from which he cannot escape. He is a hunter, a fisherman, a shepherd, or a critical critic, and must remain so if he does not want to lose his means of livelihood.' In other words, a man's productive activity is not his own in the sense that he shapes it himself. It is determined by the material and social circumstances in which he lives; and, for this reason, 'man's own deed becomes an alien power opposed to him, which enslaves him instead of being controlled by him'.[44] In modern industry, Marx continues, the bondage of man is made complete. As the productive forces of bourgeois society develop, the division of labour is refined until the activity of the worker becomes a 'single mindless operation endlessly repeated'.[45] He is deprived of even the narrow satisfaction achieved by the medieval artisan. Since the worker must work or perish, his work is performed, not freely in satisfaction of a need, but as a necessary means to an end. And herein lies the alienation of the worker from his own activity and therefore from himself, 'that the work is *external* to the worker, that it is not part of his nature; and that, consequently, he does not fulfil himself in his work but denies himself'.[46]

But if the worker, in his activity, is alienated from himself, then so is the capitalist. He too finds his activity governed by forces he does not control. As personified capital, 'he shares with the miser the passion for wealth as wealth. But that which in the miser is a mere idiosyncrasy, is, in the capitalist, the effect of the social mechanism of which he is but one of the wheels . . . the development of capitalist production makes it constantly necessary to keep increasing the amount of capital laid out in a given industrial undertaking, and competition makes the immanent laws of capitalist production to be felt by each individual capitalist as external coercive laws.'[47] The capitalist is no more a free agent than the worker, and, for this reason, he is no less exposed to the blows of fortune. But, according to Marx, there is this difference, 'that where worker and capitalist both suffer, the worker suffers in his existence while the capitalist suffers in the profit on his dead mammon'.[48]

It is, of course, no part of Marx's thesis that social activity is causally determined. He recognizes that both worker and capitalist are daily faced with choices and have to make decisions. They are, to this extent, free men. But the point is that they find themselves in a situation in which the considerations that govern their choices have nothing to do with their purposes as potentially self-determined moral individuals. The capitalist may, indeed, resign and cease to be a capitalist; but, since he must live in society if he is to live at all, he will accomplish nothing except to exchange one kind of socially determined activity for another. No matter what he does, he remains a wheel in the social mechanism.

It is in this sense that the individual is not free, but subject to necessity. Whether he is the plaything of the gods or a cog in the industrial machine, there is a discrepancy between what he knows he ought to do and what, in practice, he must do. His natural inclinations, his human self, must be set aside in order that his more imperative needs be satisfied; and thus he is made to serve a purpose other than his own. The awareness of this incoherence or absurdity endemic in practical existence inspires the demand for a morally coherent world; and this demand is, I suggest, the stuff of which political myths are made.

The Myth of the Proletarian Revolution

It is sometimes suggested that a revolution is a violent attempt to change the constitution of a society, i.e. the manner in which public offices are allocated, goods distributed and jobs divided.[49] This may be what happens in a revolution; but it is less than what the revolutionary intends. The revolutionary regards his world as one riven by a conflict so fundamental that it brooks of no compromise, and he sees the revolution, not merely as altering a particular aspect or part of his world, but as changing that world as a whole. It is, in fact, 'the ascent of man from the kingdom of necessity to the kingdom of freedom';[50] and usually it is the people themselves who are cast as the agents of their liberation. 'Revolutions,' Lenin remarked, 'are festivals of the oppressed and the exploited. At no other time are the mass of the people in a position to come forward so actively as the creators of a new social order, as at the time of revolution.'[51] In short, the idea of a revolution takes the form of a projection, an eschatological vision of a future event or state of affairs in which the present unsatisfactory world is abolished.

In practical activity, there is always an idea of the future, but it is normally a partial future, one that assumes that, though particular details may change, the general order of things will remain. It is also normally assumed that the anticipated future is a mere possibility which any unforeseen turn of events might frustrate. Practical wisdom of the everyday kind therefore consists in making conjectures based on the expectation that certain regularities observed in the past will continue to occur in the future; and, since the continued occurrence of these regularities depends on 'all other things being equal', the practical man will hedge his bets. His wisdom is founded, not on faith, but on calculation. However, eschatological or revolutionary expectations are not of this kind. They are in no sense extrapolations from existing trends; and the *eschatos* is often seen, not as a mere possibility, but as a certainty. How we may ask, are such visions formed?

If we examine their content, we will find that they contain a mirror-image of the world the myth-maker takes to be the one in which he lives.

Lactantius, for instance, found himself in a world where war, want and injustice prevailed and the righteous survived only as a dispossessed and persecuted minority. The Kingdom of Christ, by contrast, is a world in which the righteous hold sway and there is no scarcity, toil, strife or sudden death to interfere with their receiving their due rewards. The mountains drip with honey, the rivers flow with milk, the lion lies down with the lamb, and so forth. Everything is, in short, stood on its head. This is doubtlessly an extreme case, but most eschatological myths will, to some degree, display the same characteristics. It is as if the myth-maker simply inverts the present state of affairs and projects the picture thus obtained into the indeterminate future.

Sometimes, of course, the perfect world to come is made more con-crete through being identified with a state of affairs known, or believed, to have existed in the past. The Levellers and Diggers, we recall, found such a world in the ancient Anglo-Saxon constitution. They had lost this world as the result of a catastrophe, the Norman invasion; and everything that was unjust or oppressive in their present circumstances could be accounted for by the fact that the existing order was sustained only by force and for the sole purpose of securing the position of an alien ruling class. Force, however, could be met by force. And when, at last, the Norman invader was expelled, the people would retrieve the morally coherent world they had lost and would thus be restored to their liberties. But it would be wrong to suppose that the Levellers and Diggers derived their notion of the future from their knowledge of the historical past. They were not, in the main, historians. The views they held of the past were, no less than their view of the future, determined by their practical experience of the present.

We should, perhaps, remind ourselves that, if political myths con-sisted of nothing but visions of a more perfect world to come, they would not be myths. They would be Utopias. Sorel, we recall, argued that, while Utopias are descriptions of an ideal state of affairs, myths, by contrast, are expectations of a future event. It is obvious that Sorel was thinking only of eschatological myths. None the less, his point is a good one, for it emphasizes that a myth, whatever else it might be, is always a story. It is a narrative of events cast in dramatic form. A myth may, of course, contain a Utopian vision; but its definitive characteristic is that, in addition to this, it tells a story. And an eschatological myth is the story of a group destined to be involved in a cataclysmic trans-formation of the world.

In the early works of Marx, we find both a preoccupation with the problem of achieving a morally coherent world and a rudimentary vision of a future communistic society. But we find nothing that can be described as a mythical account. The Marx of the *Economic and Philosophical Manuscripts* may well have been a visionary, but he was not a mythmaker. He became a myth-maker only when he had formulated his general theory of social change and then sat down to write *The German Ideology*. For it is here that we find, for the first time, the destiny of the revolutionary proletariat set forth as a dramatically coherent sequence of events. The point is significant because it raises the question as to the relationship between political myth and social science. The two are not (as is sometimes supposed) incompatible. Sociological theories often prove, on inspection, to be little more than justifications of political myths; and, *vice versa*, political myths are often generated through the application of a sociological theory to the study of contemporary events. The latter, I suggest, was the case with Marx; and his success in thus using his theory to frame a call to action was made possible by the structure of the theory itself.

Marx starts from the point that, in order to live, men must produce their means of subsistence. The manner in which they do so does not depend on their free and arbitrary choice. They must use the tools, methods and natural resources they find at hand. The specific character of their productive activity is, therefore, determined by the material and social circumstances in which they find themselves. However, as men produce, they act upon and change their environment; they transform the wilderness into a garden or, as the case may be, the countryside into an industrial jungle. And since the conditions under which they produce have changed, the character of their productive activity must also change. Man's productive activity transforms the world and is, in turn, transformed by it.

There is a further point. Productive activity is necessarily social activity. It is an activity which men perform in co-operation with others. Society, Marx suggests, is nothing but an association of men set up for the purpose of producing the means of existence. It follows, then, that the manner in which men produce will determine the manner in which they co-operate, that 'a certain mode of production or industrial stage is always combined with a certain mode of co-operation or social stage'.[52]

Any society, Marx suggests, takes the form of a division of labour, and this entails 'the *distribution*, and indeed, the *unequal* distribution, both quantitative and qualitative, of labour and its products, hence property'.[53] Inevitably, some members of society will benefit from the prevailing relations of production and they will benefit at the expense of others. Conflict between exploiters and exploited is unavoidable. This conflict, however, is not merely a clash between self-interested groups; it is also a conflict between 'the interest of the separate individual or individual family and the communal interest of all individuals who have intercourse with one another'. And indeed, this communal interest does not exist merely in the imagination, 'but first of all in reality, as the mutual interdependence of the individuals among whom the labour is divided'.[54] In other words, although a given mode of co-operation may entail the exploitation of one part of society by another, it cannot be overthrown without the ruin of all. Its maintenance is, therefore, in the interest of society as a whole; and special measures must be taken for its protection.

The need for these measures is satisfied, in the first instance, by the state with its administration and armed forces. The state, by the use of force, defends the existing social structure with its property relations; and, in so doing, it automatically maintains the hegemony of the dominant class. It can, therefore, be described as the tool of this class, even though it may not conceive of itself as such. The communal interest is also supported by the religious, philosophical and artistic culture of the society. 'The ruling ideas are nothing more than the ideal expression of the dominant material relationships, the dominant material relationships grasped as ideas; hence of the relationships which make the one class the ruling one, therefore, the ideas of its dominance.'[55] It is, we should add, not the intention of Marx to suggest that consciousness is merely a passive reflection of reality. He tells us that 'Consciousness can never be anything else than conscious existence, and the existence of men is their actual life-process';[56] but the reverse also holds true. The existence of men can never be anything but conscious existence, and the manner in which they act is bound to be determined, in part, by their notion of the world in which they are acting. Their notion of the world may be mistaken. It may, for instance, be a notion that suggests that certain property relations are a necessary part of the natural order when, in fact, these property relations have outlived their usefulness. But, although time may reveal the notion to have been an illusion, the notion itself may retain its influence over the behaviour of men long after it has been overtaken by events.

Every economic and social system is, according to Marx, inherently subject to change; and the change tends to be uneven. As the mode of production develops, it increasingly requires, for its further development, an adjustment in the mode of co-operation and, particularly, in the prevailing property relations. At a certain point, 'the material productive forces of society come in conflict with the existing relations of production, or—what is but a legal expression for the same thing—with the property relations within which they have been at work hitherto. From forms of development of the productive forces these relations turn into their fetters. Then begins an epoch of social revolution.'[57] The interest of the old ruling class ceases to coincide with the communal interest of society as a whole; the ruling ideas lose their appearance of universal validity and become revealed as the ideology of a particular class. Meanwhile, a new class emerges which is able to present its interest as the common interest. 'It can do this because, to start with, its interest really is more connected with the common interest of all other non-ruling classes, because under the pressure of hitherto existing conditions its interest has not yet been able to develop as the particular interest of a particular class.'[58] Since the old ruling class, exploiting its monopoly of political power, uses force to maintain the now obsolete property relations, the newly emerging class uses force to seize political power and destroy the old social structure which stands in its way. 'Force,' says Marx, 'is the midwife of every old society pregnant with a new one.'[59]

This is an obviously attractive theory. It makes possible a coherent account of the interaction between the economic, social, political and cultural activities of men in society. It is capable of infinite elaboration and it is sufficiently general to be applied to the analysis of any conceivable society. Above all, it is free of any values. It is purely and simply a theory of social structure and social change. Its purpose is to explain; it prescribes nothing. Apart from the bald statement that man has to eat in order to live, it says nothing about man's moral purpose or his ultimate destiny. It voices no hopes or desires, and it implies no commitment to a cause.

But all this changes when we turn from the theory itself and consider its application to the study of a particular society. According to the theory, any society is necessarily a self-destroying system. Its history will appear as the history of a class struggle which must end 'either in a revolutionary reconstitution of society at large or in the common ruin of the contending classes'.[60] The conflict will not merely be one between abstract forces remote from the daily lives of men; it will be one in which men directly take part, and it will manifest itself in particular historical events: the French revolution, the confiscation of monastic lands, the repeal of the Corn Laws, and so forth. Such events will derive their significance from their place in the general development of society; and, since this development takes the form of a class struggle, the events themselves will be endowed with a distinctively dramatic character.

The theory has a further peculiarity. Its basic logic is such that it charts out beforehand the general course which any society must follow. A society, according to the theory, comes into being within a particular set of material circumstances. These circumstances shape the character of that society in that they determine its mode of production and the manner in which it organizes itself. They are, in effect, the material conditions of its existence. But, since no society can proceed about its business without radically altering these same conditions, it must, in time, cut the ground from under its own feet and thus hasten the day of its downfall. This, then, is the tragic destiny that haunts all historical societies: they are, each in their own way, heroes whose very triumph makes their doom inevitable.

With regard to societies other than his own, the Marxist theoretician can sit back and behold with sardonic indifference the spectacle of a tragedy endlessly repeated. But, when he considers his own society, he is less comfortably placed. His theory commands him to envisage the present state of affairs as an episode in the drama of a world torn by contradictions. The end of the drama, he knows, can only be the revolutionary transformation of society into something totally new. Whatever affection he might feel for the existing order is, therefore, qualified by his awareness that it bears the mark of Cain. It is founded on the ruins of a previous order, and it will, in time, suffer the same fate. The expropriators will be expropriated. Moreover, the stress historical materialism lays upon the role of 'mental production' in the revolutionary transformation of society compels the theorist to consider his own practical position with regard to the events he contemplates. He cannot exclude himself from his own analysis, and this means that his scholarly detachment must go by the board. He must either keep silent or confess his commitment. In short, although the theory is not itself a political myth, it is such that, when applied to the study of the world in which we live, it cannot but produce a narrative of events in dramatic form complete with the projection of an end to come; and the theorist himself becomes a revolutionary myth-maker, a prophet of impending catastrophe.

Marx himself argued that the proletarian revolution would be the revolution to end all revolutions. It would result, not in yet another class-divided society, but in a classless society where men could, at last, achieve both justice and freedom. We cannot here review the considerations that led Marx to this interesting conclusion. Suffice it to say that he reached it, not by a feat of imagination, but through the systematic application of his general theory to the conditions prevailing in nineteenth-century Europe. This does not, of course, make it any the less a political myth. It is (as I have already argued) not its origin that makes a particular doctrine a myth, but its dramatic structure and the fact that it is used in practical argument. Nor is the myth of the proletariat the only myth of our time to be inspired by otherwise innocuous academic achievements. We need but consider the doctrines spawned by the application of Darwinist theory to the study of political history to find several myths formed in a fashion analogous to that which I have ascribed to Marx.

Chapter Five

Ideology and political myths

Part of the reason why political myths have attracted so little attention in the academic world is that they are usually deployed together with other and more familiar kinds of discourse. They get, so to speak, lost in the wood, and it is easy to see how this can happen. Although the myth-maker possesses, in his myth, a simple and persuasive argument, the cultural context in which he operates is often extremely complex. His account will inevitably deal with matters touched upon also by philosophers, historians and scientists; and he will find it urged against him that what he asserts to be true (from the standpoint of his myth) is scientifically, historically or philosophically false. It is, therefore, not surprising that he should feel unable to leave well enough alone. If he is to persuade his audience, he must show that his message is consistent with the prevailing culture of his time; and thus he will be drawn into controversies which have nothing mythical about them. The result is, as often as not, that he incorporates his myth into the framework of a general ideology.

In doing so, he may, of course, lose as much as he gains. Sorel, in his *Materials for a Theory of the Proletariat*, observes that the medieval prophets of the Millennium made a fundamental error when they abandoned the realm of imagination in order to 'philosophize', for this enabled the Church to refute their theories and condemn them as heretics. It is in this connection that Sorel defines an ideology as a myth which has been rationalized and thus laid open for discussion.[1] Though a full enquiry into the subject would take us too far afield, we may usefully regard an ideology as a heterogeneous collection of practical beliefs which have been reduced to a system through being interpreted in the light of a single key doctrine; and we may profit from Sorel's suggestion to the extent of agreeing that this key doctrine is often (though not always) a political myth. But this raises a question. How are political myths related to the various doctrines with which they are thus associated? And, in particular, can a mythical argument be translated into, or replaced by, some other kind of argument?

According to Bultmann, it can. The New Testament, he tells us, presents the fundamentals of the Christian faith in a mythical language which is now dangerously obsolete. 'It is impossible to use electric light and the wireless and to avail ourselves of modern medicine and surgical discoveries, and at the same time to believe in the New Testament world of dæmons and spirits.' The New Testament must, therefore, be demythologized. This, Bultmann suggests, can be done without in any way damaging the faith for, in the end, 'the importance of the New Testament mythology lies not in its imagery but in the understanding of existence which it enshrines'. And such an understanding can perfectly well be stated in the non-mythical terms appropriate to modern man.[2] To this Jaspers replies that Bultmann has seriously misconceived the nature of myth. Myth, he says, 'is not a cloak or disguise put over a general idea, which can be better and more directly grasped intellectually'. It is, on the contrary, a carrier of meanings which can be expressed in no other way. Myths are untranslatable. 'They cannot be interpreted rationally; they are interpreted only by new myths, by being transformed. Myths interpret each other.'[3]

Jaspers does, however, concede the main point. While denying that myths can be translated into philosophical dissertations, he agrees that the true meaning of a myth is not its literal meaning. A myth may well be a plain account of events, but this plain account is to be understood as a code in which things transcendent and 'unconditional' are expressed. In short, Bultmann's error lies, not in assuming that myths contain timeless truths, but in thinking that these truths can be expressed in non-mythical terms.

I have already discussed the defects of the view that myths contain hidden meanings, and I will labour the point no further. However, the suggestion that mythical arguments cannot be translated into philosophical or scientific statements calls for closer examination. Myth does, after all, resemble both philosophy and science in one important respect: it is a mode of explanation. The ripening of the corn may be explained by reference to the story of Persephone and her annual return to earth in accordance with an agreement made between Hades and Demeter; the Punic Wars may be understood as the culmination of a feud which began with Aeneas's betrayal of Dido; or the existence of so unsatisfactory an institution as copyhold may be accounted for by the fact that it was imposed on the people to serve the interests of an alien conqueror. All these are mythical explanations. They explain something by telling the story of how it came about. As Rose observes, 'Asked why it rains, scientist and myth-maker alike can give an answer.'[4] And the answer a myth-maker gives is in terms of a story.

This, however, is not sufficient to make mythical thinking a primitive kind of philosophy or science. Philosophy and science explain things, not by telling the story of how they came about, but by subsuming them under general laws and principles. Moreover, they aspire, with moderate success, to truth and objectivity; they aim at providing knowledge for its own sake. A mythical explanation does nothing of the kind. The understanding it provides is a practical understanding; that is to say, an understanding in which men consider the world that confronts them, not as the object of disinterested curiosity, but as the material for their activity. In their effort to understand this world of *pragmata*, of things endowed with moral or utilitarian value, men view their circumstances in the light of their purposes, and their explanations are simultaneously justifications or prescriptions. No doubt, some distortion of fact does occur. But, when practical considerations are foremost, men tend to believe what, at that moment, they find it convenient or necessary to believe. Indeed, the notion that academic standards are always more important than the achievement of peace, prosperity and justice is a scholar's conceit which, when it comes to the crunch, scholars themselves are the first to abandon.

It may be that, precisely because of its dramatic form, a mythical argument accentuates the distortion of fact endemic in practical thinking. But the difference is one of degree, not of kind. It does not, as some have supposed, elevate myth to the status of poetic fiction; nor does it mean that the myth-maker deliberately departs from the truth in order to make his point. Indeed, it is plain that, if a myth is to be a practical argument, the chief condition for its success is that it be understood as a true narrative of events. If it is regarded as a pack of lies, it may well provide entertainment, but it will fail as an explanation and it will lack prescriptive force. Myths no longer believed to be true may, of course, survive in a culture as the material for artistic or literary invention; but they are, strictly speaking, dead or obsolete myths. A living myth is invariably intended as a *vera narratio*, a plain account of what actually happened.

This brings us to the kind of discourse with which myth is most likely to be confused, namely, history. It is evident that, in the view of myth I am recommending, much that passes for history is properly speaking myth or is shot through with mythical ways of thought. But there is a significant difference. Although a history is like a myth in that it is intended as a true narrative, the reasons why historical statements are believed to be true are not the same as those that hold for mythical statements. A historian persuades us to accept his assertions by citing the relevant evidence: official documents, eye-witness reports, archaeological finds and so forth. Furthermore, he tries to show that his assertions are, not only reasonable inferences from the evidence, but also consistent with other conclusions reached concerning the same period or sequence of events. The myth-maker proceeds in a different fashion altogether. The view of the world that we find in a myth is always a practical view. Its aim is either to advocate a certain course of action or to justify acceptance of an existing state of affairs. Myths are, therefore, believed to be true, not because the historical evidence is compelling, but because they make sense of men's present experience. They tell the story of how it came about. And events are selected for inclusion in a myth, partly because they coincide with what men think *ought* to have happened, and partly because they are consistent with the drama as a whole.

It is clear that the myth-maker can decide which events to include in his account only if he knows the story from beginning to end. This presents no difficulty if, as is often the case, he simply identifies the end with the present state of affairs. The conclusion is thus given, and he can construct his account by selecting those events which, in retrospect, can be seen to have advanced the action to its predestined end. And, if an event looms so large in the memory of his audience that it cannot be omitted, then it can always be refashioned in the telling so that it fits into the general drift of the story. It goes without saying that the more the myth-maker can rely on traditional beliefs and established historical truths the better. But if his story requires a few details for which there is no such backing, he can supply them himself and still expect to be believed. There are, no doubt, limits to the scope of his invention. He cannot positively deny what his audience knows to have happened, and he cannot assert what they regard as being completely impossible. His account must be at least a plausible story—even if it need be no more than just that. But if it is indeed a plausible story and if it casts real light on the experience of its audience, then it is likely to be received as a true account, regardless of what the professional historian might say.

In many myths, however, the present state of affairs is regarded, not as the end of the story, but as a stage on the way. This poses a problem. In order to construct his account, the myth-maker must know the conclusion; but how can he know what has not yet occurred? I have already discussed certain aspects of this question. Here I wish only to add a general point. It is often argued that, since what happened in the past cannot now be changed, the past offers, as it were, a field of fixed facts concerning which we can establish the truth. Future events are, by contrast, a matter for speculation. There are no future facts. What men believe concerning the future must be derived from their present experience and is consequently subject to constant change. The difficulty with this thesis is that it applies (if at all) only to the professional historian. For most men, the past is as dark and as fluid as the future, and what they believe about the past is determined in much the same way as their ideas about the future, namely, by inference from their present practical experience.

It is important to stress that a myth is always told from the standpoint of the present, for this carries the implication that, as the circumstances in which men find themselves change, so they reconstruct their myths. The same is said to hold for history—and so indeed it does, but not in the same way. The myth-maker reshapes his account of the past because a change in his circumstances has brought about a corresponding change in his practical position. The historian does so because new evidence has come to light or because he considers previous accounts to be based on an incorrect interpretation of the existing evidence. It is true that, in interpreting the evidence, the historian must have recourse to generalizations which he can get only from the cultural milieu in which he moves. He is, like everyone else, a creature of his time. But it does not follow that his purpose is to preach a sermon. Where the historian deploys current knowledge in an attempt to elucidate the past, the myth-maker does so in order to make a point of practical importance to his contemporaries. And between the two there is a world of difference.

Myth, then, is neither history, philosophy nor science; and there is no proper sense in which a mythical account can be translated into a philosophical, scientific or historical statement. To this extent, Jaspers has a point. However, the fact that (for instance) a scientific statement is scientific does not mean to say that it cannot be used in a practical argument. Its scientific character depends, not on its logical structure, but on the way it is understood and on the context in which it is used. And the same goes for historical and philosophical statements. There is, therefore, nothing to prevent the myth-maker from converting scientific, philosophical and historical statements into practical arguments and thus integrating them into the framework of an ideology. Indeed, we have seen that he frequently does just that.

But the question still remains as to the relationship between a political myth and the other kinds of practical argument with which it may be associated. Despite my strictures against the reading of abstract profundities into practical arguments, it is a fact that, in their practice, men often view themselves as acting in the light of eternally valid principles. They wish their deeds to be possessed of a significance that is more than merely temporal, and they plunge themselves into practical affairs in the hope of finding some way to overcome the destructiveness of time. It might, of course, be said that all such hopes are vain, that, in the nature of the case, practical activity aims at achieving something particular in a specific set of circumstances, and that its significance is therefore both limited and transient. But this view, though correct, conceals the real complexity of practical thought. Let us consider an example.

Cicero, we recall, wished to restore popular confidence in the republican constitution of Rome. To this end, he advanced two markedly different arguments. Firstly, he maintained that the present constitution was the one originally established by the founder-heroes of the republic and that the Roman people could maintain their position only by remaining faithful to the principles that had inspired the foundation. And secondly he argued, on theoretical grounds, that the only constitution sufficiently free of structural defects to survive indefinitely was a mixed constitution of the kind that Rome was lucky enough to possess.

The first argument is mythical in character, and, like all mythical arguments, its point is historically specific. It appeals directly to the Roman people and to no one else; and its message makes sense only in the context of the constitutional crisis that preceded the principate of Augustus Caesar. The second argument, however, is capable of a more general application. It rests on a theory concerning the relationship between constitutional structure and political stability, and it applies, in principle, to any political society at any time. Yet Cicero uses it to make exactly the same practical point he makes in the first argument. Indeed, the two arguments support and interpret each other. The myth supplies the theoretical argument with a concrete reference and a temporal perspective it would otherwise lack; and the theoretical argument endows the myth with academic respectability and a certain timelessly abstract significance.

This simultaneous deployment of mythical and non-mythical arguments is so common that we must regard it as the rule rather than the exception. The Church Fathers, for instance, found it necessary to justify their account of man's fall and redemption by theorizing about the nature of substance and the immortality of the soul; the Huguenots and the Levellers combined their appeals to the mythical past with a range of arguments based on the principles of natural right; and the National Socialists looked to modern genetics and Darwinian biology for a vindication of their racial doctrines. In all these cases, it would be fair to say that the myths are interpreted by and, in a sense, translated into arguments of a non-mythical kind. There may well be cultures so rudimentary that myth is the only available form of practical argument; and we may suppose that, in such cultures, myths are indeed 'interpreted only by new myths'. But this is not because myths are inherently untranslatable. It is because there is nothing into which they can be translated. In any reasonably civilized society, myths are incorporated into a general ideology composed of several mutually supporting practical points of view. And, if we wonder why the myth-maker resorts to myths when he has more sophisticated tools at hand, the answer is that, although he doubts whether his mythical argument can stand alone, he regards it as being more lucid and compelling than an argument from abstract principles.

Political myths and practical activity

In his practice, the individual sets himself goals and deliberates about the means to achieve them. Having freely chosen to do what he does, he can take the credit for his accomplishments and regard his life as the progressive actualization of his individual gifts and aspirations. Or so he can, if he finds himself living in a morally coherent world. If, however, he finds himself in a morally incoherent world, then his practical activity assumes a different character altogether. For here, as we have seen, the individual is, to some degree, constrained to act according to necessity; and, in so far as this is the case, his deeds are not his own, and it becomes questionable whether he can be regarded as responsible for their consequences.

The medieval moralists took the view that, when a man acts as the instrument of a purpose greater than his own, then the rules that govern his conduct as an individual cease to apply. As Augustine put it: 'Those men do not break the commandment·which forbids killing, who make war by the authority of God's command, or being in some place of public magistracy, put to death malefactors according to their laws. . . .'[5] And John of Salisbury later elaborated the point in his *Policraticus*. As far as regards public matters, he tells us, the prince has no will of his own 'apart from that which the law or equity enjoins or the calculation of the common interest requires'. The prince, indeed, is 'the minister of the common interest', and nothing he does in the exercise of his office can be construed as a personal act. He is the passionless instrument of the body politic and, as such, 'he bears a sword wherewith he sheds blood blamelessly, without becoming thereby a man of blood'.[6]

We can, then, distinguish between a man's public duty and his private morality. And John of Salisbury's point is that to introduce the rules appropriate to the one into the performance of the other is to invite confusion and disaster. The maintenance of society depends on men being able to keep personal considerations separate from their public duty. The magistrate must do things he would never dream of doing as a private individual; and he must be able to do them with a clear conscience and without risk of retribution. We might say that, in performing his public duty, he achieves a practical existence which places him outside the realm of mere morality. His actions are not, for this reason, beyond all criticism. He simply finds himself in a practical world governed by standards and purposes different from those which apply to the private individual. If a moral wrong is committed, then the blame must fall, not on him, but on the body politic whose instrument he is. What he does in his public capacity is justified, not because it is morally good, but because it is socially or politically necessary. He did not make the world in which he finds himself, and he did not write the terms of reference which define his office. He is personally not to blame.

However, the matter is not quite so straightforward. The standards that govern the performance of a man's public duty may differ from those that apply to his private life, but they are not wholly irrelevant to one another. As the Christian moralists stressed, no man can serve two masters if the one commands what the other forbids. In entering the realm of public activity, the individual is freed from the obligation to obey the commands of his moral self—but he does not cease to hear these commands. What he says and does in public is not what his inner voice says and bids him do. He is one man, yet he lives two morally incompatible lives.

This brings us back to the myth-maker. When he denounces the established practices of the society in which he lives, he is claiming that these practices conflict with the private practice of a substantial part of that society. In his view, the arrangements his society has adopted for the management of its common affairs fail to harmonize with the manner in which its members live, or feel they ought to live. A serious contradiction has emerged. Men are prevented from pursuing their legitimate ends. Their own society works against them in such a way as to frustrate their aspirations and deny them the kind of life they feel is rightly theirs.

Like the magistrate, the revolutionary myth-maker thinks of himself as having a public duty which is distinct from, and may conflict with, the principles that guide his private life. His public duty is, to be sure, conceived differently. He regards himself as an actor on the stage of world history rather than as a wheel in the social mechanism or an organ in the body politic. But the effect is the same. As Regis Debray remarked at his trial in Bolivia, the individuals engaged in a revolutionary war 'are but mere representatives of two irreconcilable orders'. The war itself is the fruit of social, economic and moral antagonisms which precede the individual and exist independently of him. He is personally innocent; yet it is he who is killed. And herein lies the tragedy. 'It is not individuals that are placed face to face in these battles, but class interests and ideas; but those who fall in them, those who die, are persons, are men. We cannot avoid this contradiction, escape from this pain.'[7] In a morally incoherent world, the revolutionary, no less than the magistrate, finds himself in a predicament from which he can extricate himself only by an appeal to necessity. He must, like the magistrate, declare that the end justifies the means. But, in his case, the end is, not the maintenance of an existing system, but the achievement of a future state of affairs, and he believes the advent of this state of affairs to be predetermined, just as the magistrate takes the existing system to be necessary or natural.

It is often said that determinist beliefs lead to quietism in politics. All political activity, it is argued, consists in trying to bring about a change for the better or to prevent a change for the worse.[8] But where men are convinced that God, Fate or History have already decided the issue, they are content to sit back and let things take their course. In fact, however, men often behave quite differently. Orthodox Calvinists and Marxists have not, in the past, been noted for their quietist approach to public affairs, despite the distinctively determinist character of their beliefs. And the reason is not far to seek. Practical men of a determinist stamp do not regard themselves as attempting to change the world. They see themselves as the willing instruments of a purpose higher than their own, and they view their practical activity as a service and a performance. 'I am,' said Cromwell, 'a poor weak creature, and not worthy the name of a worm; yet accepted to serve the Lord and his People.'[9] The abiding consideration of such men is to adjust themselves to the power that governs the world. They have no enterprise of their own to be accomplished, for (to quote Cromwell again) 'all this is none other than the work of God'.[10] Instead, they have a role to be performed. They neither change nor preserve; they merely participate.

The Romans, we recall, displayed a similar approach to practical activity. Military service or public office provided the opportunity, not to change the world, but to put on a distinguished performance. The fact that, for example, the outcome of a battle was preordained—and the Romans rarely fought unless the auspices were favourable—would tell the individual soldier very little about his lot. Fortune might bring him death even in victory. But this was of minor importance, for his aim was not so much to win the battle as to play his part and thus to make the victory his own.

It is evident that the question of responsibility cannot be separated from the problem of identity. In practical activity, a man must consider, among other things, whether the action he proposes to take is appropriate to the kind of person he conceives himself to be. If he is to perform his role, he must know what character he is supposed to play; and it is by defining his character, by establishing his identity, that he delimits the area of his responsibility.

If the revolutionary myth-maker is, like John of Salisbury's prince, to shed blood blamelessly, then he must sink his individuality into the identity of a greater whole. He must regard himself as the representative of the group or movement whose cause he has espoused. There is, of course, a sense in which this increases rather than diminishes his responsibility; for, while his deeds become those of the group, the deeds of the group become, by the same token, *his* deeds, irrespective of whether he is personally involved or not. 'As a revolutionary,' says Debray, 'I feel and I declare myself jointly responsible for all the "crimes" committed by all revolutionaries everywhere in the world, from the printing of fliers to attacks on banks to obtain funds, from illegal meetings to the execution of torturers.'[11] We note that it is not as a moral individual that Debray claims the credit or takes the blame for things done by his fellow revolutionaries. Indeed, he stresses that he speaks 'as a revolutionary'. The moral 'I', the 'grammatical fiction' as Koestler's Rubashov describes it, is absent and remains untouched. So far as the revolutionary is concerned, his real self is an abstract person. He is the representative of a collectivity, the bearer of an idea. He is the word made flesh.

Cassirer, we recall, claimed it as a distinguishing feature of mythical thought that the part is identified with the whole, the individual with the species to which he belongs. Certainly, nothing is more common in political argument. Everywhere, the sins of the fathers are visited on the sons. A Jew commits a crime and the whole race stands condemned; the nation wins a war and the individual citizen feels himself enhanced, though personally he never fired a shot. In this way of reasoning, no man is a mere individual. He is the representative of his group, and he embodies in himself all the attributes which others, rightly or wrongly, ascribe to that group. Cassirer is, of course, mistaken in supposing that this kind of reasoning obtains only in mythical thought. But it is true that, without this kind of reasoning, it becomes impossible to view the world mythically. If the Romans had not been able to identify themselves with the founder heroes of the old republic, the story of the foundation would have lacked any practical significance. Communists in Western Europe would have been unmoved by the achievement of Lenin had they not regarded it as the achievement of the proletariat as a class. Mythical thought is, in short, a way of practical reasoning that presupposes a readiness to identify the particular with the general, the part with the whole.

Normally, the myth-maker acquires the content of his collective identity of self-image by reference to precedents established in the past. Reporting on a visit to Cuba, Michael Frayn writes: 'I was very struck by the behaviour of a weedy young party official who showed me round a new agricultural project in Pinar del Rio. . . . He kept throwing colossal bone-cracking handshakes and spine-jarring slaps on the back to anyone who came within range, and from time to time doubling up over an imaginary sub-machine gun and spraying imaginary bullets into the surrounding undergrowth. He was 25, and he was playing *guerrilleros*.' The *guerrilleros* had, of course, long since become ministers of state, and the heroic period of the Cuban Revolution had passed into legend; but, as legend, it survived to provide an interpretation of the present and a guide to the future. 'The austerity of life in the Sierra lends significance and purpose to the austerity of life today. The constant watchfulness which a guerrilla band must maintain against ambush and treachery explains the constant "revolutionary vigilance" which is urged now. The concreteness of the enemy in the Sierra makes concrete the notion of a present counter-revolutionary enemy.'[12]

Frayn was, evidently, observing the effects of a typical foundation myth. And, indeed, it is where the revolution or war of national liberation is already achieved that the myth-maker can most easily shape his public identity and define his role. His predecessors are known and their accomplishments serve as a paradigm for his present activity. But the myth-maker who still has his revolution to make is in a different position. The dramatic crisis in terms of which he defines his role lies, not in the past, but in the future; and, however confident he may be that the revolution is inevitable, the fact remains that neither he nor anyone else has trod that particular path before. He has no precedents to guide his steps. His role is, accordingly, ill-defined, and the temptation is great to disregard the uniqueness of the drama in which he is engaged and to seek guidance from previous but similar dramas.

'The tradition of all the dead generations,' says Marx, 'weighs like a nightmare on the brain of the living. And just when they seem engaged in revolutionizing themselves and things . . . they anxiously conjure up the spirits of the past to their service and borrow from them names, battle cries and costumes in order to present the new scene of world history in this time-honoured disguise and this borrowed language.' Such a use of the past, he continues, can only mislead; but sometimes the deception is necessary. The men of the French Revolution 'performed the task of their time in Roman costume and with Roman phrases, the task of unchaining and setting up modern *bourgeois* society'. Once the task was done, the bourgeoisie forgot that 'ghosts from the days of Rome had watched over its cradle' and settled down to the more mundane business of getting rich. 'But unheroic as bourgeois society is, it nevertheless took heroism, sacrifice, terror, civil war and battles of peoples to bring it into being. And in the classically austere traditions of the Roman republic its gladiators found the ideals and the art forms, the self-deceptions that they needed in order to conceal from themselves the bourgeois limitations of the contents of their struggles and to keep their enthusiasm on the high plane of the great historical tragedy.' The proletarian revolution, Marx adds, will require no such deceptions. 'It cannot begin with itself before it has stripped off all superstition in regard to the past. Earlier revolutions required recollections of past world history in order to drug themselves concerning their own content. In order to arrive at its own content, the revolution of the nineteenth century must let the dead bury their dead.'[13]

The problem, however, still remains. According to Marx, the proletariat 'cannot draw its poetry from the past, but only from the future'. But the future has no content of its own and, therefore, lacks the material for the kind of poetry the revolutionary requires if he is to define his role. 'No man,' says Hobbes, 'can have in his mind a conception of the future, for the future is not yet. But of our conceptions of the past, we make a future.'[14] In the end, the only protection the revolutionary has against being misled by the past is his own ignorance. It was, as Debray remarks, the good fortune of Castro and his companions that none of them had read the works of Mao Tse-tung.[15]

Illusion and deception in political myths

A political myth, I have suggested, purports to be a plain account of events. It is a story told with a view to promoting some practical purpose, and it is successful only in so far as it is believed to be a true story. This does not, of course, exclude the possibility that, in advancing a mythical argument, the myth-maker either deceives himself or deliberately sets out to deceive his audience. A myth may well be believed to be true by those among whom it circulates; but this does not prevent it from being, in actual fact, a set of extravagant illusions.

Marx, as we have just seen, suggests that the men of the French Revolution dressed their actions in a heroic disguise in order to conceal the true nature of their enterprise. Had they frankly confessed to themselves and to their followers that their real purpose was to create the conditions in which bourgeois trade and industry might flourish, they would never have been able to act with the zeal and enthusiasm which the task demanded.

This seems, at first glance, a plausible explanation as to why men deceive themselves with myths. But, on closer inspection, we find that it suffers from a serious defect. If the desire for financial gain was, of itself, an insufficient inducement to rebel, then the men of the French Revolution must have been inspired by additional considerations; for instance, by a desire to achieve for themselves and their countrymen a free republic on the model of ancient Rome. It is difficult to see why the second motive should be deemed any less real than the first. It may well be that the men of the French Revolution accomplished less than they hoped. A free republic was not, in fact, established. But this does not mean that they must, therefore, have deceived themselves as to their true intentions. All it implies is that they incorrectly calculated the consequences of their actions. The difficulty with Marx's thesis is that it assumes the operation of 'real' intentions as distinct from the conscious or stated intentions of the actors involved; and, as I have argued before, such an assumption can be sustained only by postulating a superhuman agent which employs mere human beings as the unwitting instruments of its purpose. There can, I think, be little doubt that Marx himself would have been the first to repudiate any such notion.

Another suggestion is that, in their myths, men project upon the outside world conflicts that actually take place in the depths of their unconscious psyche and that this causes them to misrepresent the objective character of the circumstances in which they find themselves. According to Norman Cohn, for instance, no interpretation of popular millennialism or of totalitarian movements can ignore the psychic content of the fantasies that inspired them. 'The megalomaniac view of oneself as the Elect, wholly good, abominably persecuted yet assured of ultimate triumph; the attribution of gigantic and demonic power to the adversary;

the refusal to accept the ineluctable limitations and imperfections of human existence, such as transience, dissention, conflict, fallibility whether intellectual or moral; the obsession with inerrable prophecies— these attitudes are symptoms which together constitute the unmistakable syndrome of paranoia.' And, to support his point, he remarks that 'a paranoiac delusion does not cease to be so because it is shared by many individuals, nor yet because those individuals have real and ample grounds for regarding themselves as victims of oppression. What is decisive is that objective situations of a given type are constantly interpreted in terms of psychic conflicts which themselves remain unconscious; so that the interpretations are systematised misinterpretations, always gross and often grotesque.'[16]

Cohn, we note, does not make the mistake of asserting that myths have a hidden meaning. So far as he is concerned, they mean what the myth-maker intends them to mean. All he says is that myths give a grotesquely distorted account of reality because the myth-maker and his audience are afflicted with a psychological disorder. It is true that the definitions of psychological syndromes are often too vague to be useful and that paranoia is notoriously a case in point. None the less, the suggestion has considerable merit, and what I have to say is more of a general caution than a direct criticism.

Historians generally stand at some distance from the events and conditions on which they comment. This allows them to adopt an attitude of detached reflection and to see things in a broad perspective. But it does not endow them with a practical insight superior to that of the man on the spot. Men engaged in practical affairs certainly think; but it is a mistake to imagine that the aim of their thinking is to obtain a balanced assessment of the facts. A man confronted with the prospect of death, disgrace or serious deprivation is not easily persuaded to see the other fellow's point of view; nor is he likely to engage in edifying reflections on the limitations and imperfections of human existence. What he requires is the confidence to act, and, as often as not, this confidence is best induced by his holding the firm conviction that his cause is just and is certain to emerge victorious. In looking for evidence to support this conviction, he may, indeed, delude himself as to the objective nature of his circumstances. But he need not be a paranoid; and, in any case, there is a sense in which his interpretation of the situation is more 'realistic' than the *ex post facto* reflections of the scholar ensconced in his study. Let us take an example from what is, by now, familiar ground.

According to the Roman Foundation Myth, Romulus had a semi-divine status in that he was the son of Mars. We may suppose that the contemporaries of Naevius took this to be a plain statement of fact. But what about Cicero and the sophisticated coterie of nobles to whom he addressed himself? In his *Republic*, Cicero has this to say about Romulus: 'He was the son of Mars, for we may grant that much to the popular tradition, especially as it is not only very ancient, but has been wisely handed down by our ancestors, who desired that those who have deserved well of the commonwealth should be deemed actual descendants of the gods.' (*Rep.*, ii, 4.) And Livy makes a similar point. 'It is,' he says, 'the privilege of antiquity to mingle divine things with human, and so to add dignity to the beginnings of cities; and if any people ought to be allowed to consecrate their origins and refer them to a divine source, so great is the military glory of the Roman people that when they profess that the father of their founder was none other than Mars, the nations of the earth may as well submit to this with as good a grace as they submit to Rome's dominion.' (Livy, I, 7.)

It would appear that Cicero and Livy are being less than candid. The statement that Romulus was the son of Mars is a statement of fact and, as such, it is either true or false. Clearly, Cicero and Livy believe that it is false; yet they refuse to say so in plain terms. Part of the reason is, no doubt, the respect they both profess for traditions of great antiquity. But more important than this is their view that these ancient traditions often contain useful fictions and that useful fictions should be preserved.

We may, of course, take this as evidence for the readiness of a ruling class to maintain its position by peddling lies. But this would be doing both Cicero and Livy less than justice, for it ascribes to them an excessively academic notion of what constitutes the truth. Cicero frequently depicts the Romans of his day as being suspicious of Greek academic speculation, not on the ground that they doubted it might lead to the truth, but on the ground that they did not think the truth it led to worth having. Indeed, this is, at bottom, the attitude that Cicero himself takes. If philosophy is to be justified at all, it must be justified by its utility. And, for all his talk about history as the mistress of truth, it is the effect a historical account may have on the behaviour of men that chiefly interests him. To his mind, the canons of historiography are not the only criteria for determining the truth about past events. A particular statement may well be historically true; but, if acceptance of it leads men to act contrary to their material or moral welfare then it is, from the standpoint of practice, false. Far better than men should believe historical or philosophical falsehoods that lead them to act truly. Persistent popular traditions can, therefore, not be dismissed as the follies of a superstitious multitude merely because they are not confirmed by the results of historical research; they find their justification in the moral and political truths they imply.

. We can complicate the matter even further. Tradition had it that, shortly after the founding of the city, the Roman people found themselves worsted in battle with the Sabines. In the middle of the panic, Romulus vowed a temple to Jupiter if he would stay the flight of the army. Jupiter duly intervened; the Romans rallied their forces and returned to win a decisive victory. Some centuries later, a temple to Jupiter the Stayer was built in fulfilment of Romulus's promise.

This is the kind of tale we would expect Cicero, the critical historian, to view with a grain of salt. However, when Catiline's bid for power came to a head, Cicero found himself addressing the Senate assembled for the occasion in none other than the temple of Jupiter the Stayer. Assuming that the published version of his oration corresponds to what he said, he concluded by making a dramatic appeal to Jupiter and called upon the god to repel and destroy the forces of Catiline thus saving the city as he had saved it before.[17]

Chances are that, in the tranquillity of his study, Cicero would have hesitated to affirm his belief in the story of Jupiter and the staying of the flight. But it is most unlikely that, in a crisis which threatened not only his life but the very existence of the republic, he could have invoked the episode with anything less than complete conviction. Cicero, I suggest, felt and believed that Jupiter the Stayer was a living reality, and he believed it because, at that moment, he needed to believe it.

It is possible that there was, in Cicero's appeal to Jupiter, an element of make-believe. Make-believe is the state of mind of a man who is not merely deceived but chooses to be deceived. He makes himself a willing dupe; and he does so by placing himself in a situation which prescribes a certain well-defined role to play. As Huizinga points out, it is in games that the phenomenon of make-believe is most fully apparent.[18] But we find it also in other spheres of activity. Indeed, wherever rules and precedents govern the actions of men, their intercourse may easily assume the aspect of a game. And myths, because they cast the content of experience in dramatic form, lend themselves particularly well to the production of make-believe. However, the close association of make-believe with games should not lead us to suppose that it is always conducted in a spirit of light-hearted playfulness. The passions sometimes aroused among the participants in a game of monopoly are sufficient evidence to the contrary. And where the 'game' is one that involves matters of genuine practical import, then make-believe is conducted in a spirit of deadly earnest.

By attaining the position of consul with the support of the conservative nobility, Cicero had placed himself in a position where he had a clearly defined role to play. This role demanded that he defend the established constitution and that, in so doing, he display the austere virtues embodied in the *mos maiorum*—including the virtue of superstitious piety. It was this quality he displayed so dramatically when he invoked the aid of Jupiter the Stayer. He was, we may say, playing the part of an antique Roman; but, spurred on by the greatness of the occasion and the seriousness of the issues at stake, he played the part so well that, for a moment, he convinced himself.

To suggest (as one might) that Cicero suffered from megalomania and that this caused him to lose his grip on reality is to make the kind of mistake historians often make when they exceed their terms of reference. History is, of course, an attempt to achieve a critical understanding of past events. In this attempt, the historian can legitimately point to factors of which the men at the time he is discussing were completely unaware. What he cannot do is criticize these men for having failed to see things as he sees them. For such criticism implies the untenable view that history is a form of practical wisdom and that men of action can usefully conduct their affairs according to the rules that govern historical research. In practice, the world is viewed, not with scholarly detachment, but from the standpoint of men who have to do what, for one reason or another, they feel to be necessary. Any account of the past which confirms the necessity of the action they have in mind is, for that reason alone, deemed to be a true account. It is, in other words, the validity of men's present purposes that validates their view of the past. And though their selection of facts and their interpretations of them may differ from those of the historian, this does not mean that either they or the historian have deluded themselves. All it means is that they are engaged in different enterprises.

Political myth

We must now draw together a few of the threads. The most obvious and perhaps the most significant observation we can make about myth is that a myth is always a story, a narrative of events in dramatic form. It has a protagonist, and it has a plot with a beginning, a middle and an end. The well-known myths of the Greeks are clearly stories, and so are the various political myths we have discussed. This, however, does not mean that myths are the product of pure fantasy. Some myths do, of course, relate events which never occured. But many myths, and especially political myths, deal with people who really existed and with events that actually took place. We may disagree with the account they give of these people and events, but they are not fiction. For the most part, the myth-maker does not invent his facts; he interprets facts that are already given in the culture to which he belongs. What marks his account as being a myth is, not its content, but its dramatic form and the fact that it serves as a practical argument. Its success as a practical argument depends on its being accepted as true, and it is generally accepted as true if it explains the experience of those to whom it is addressed and justifies the practical purposes they have in mind.

This view of myth is not entirely uncontroversial, but it is one to which most contemporary mythologists would subscribe. And it has the further advantage that it enables us to distinguish myths, not only from other kinds of practical discourse, but also from the various types of story with which it is frequently confused. Fairy-tales, for instance, are unlike myths in that they are known to be fictitious and are told for amusement rather than edification. Parables and fables, on the other hand, are similar to myths in being stories told for the sake of making a practical point; but their purpose is to illustrate a moral precept or maxim, and this can be done perfectly well by telling an obviously fictitious story.

A political myth, as I understand it, is one which tells the story of a political society. In many cases, it is the story of a political society that existed or was created in the past and which must now be restored or preserved. In other cases, it concerns a political society destined to be created in the future, and it is told for the purpose of encouraging men to hasten its advent. However, a political society is not always seen as a thing to be desired. Many societies which are governed politically (rather than despotically) include groups who are either excluded from politics altogether or who find their participation so regulated as to be ineffective. Such groups may well decide that they cannot hope to achieve freedom or security until politics as such is abolished; and there are many myths which, in one way or another, express this view. (The Christian Myth of the Millennium and the German Myth of the Aryan Race are cases in point.) Myths of this kind should perhaps be called anti-political rather than political. None the less, they do deal with the fate of a political society, and, for this reason, they have found a place in our study.

A political myth does not, of course, have to be addressed to people already in a political society. In fact, political myths often find their audience among people who think of themselves as having lost a political society or as having not yet gained one; and the kind of activity such myths prescribe is therefore rarely political activity. Any group that aspires to a political existence, or which hopes to abolish it, may think of its predicament in terms of a political myth; and the kind of activity they regard as appropriate may include migration, conspiracy, revolt and war. In short, a political myth may, without contradiction, be the story of a group of people who do not constitute a political society and who do not engage in political activities.

Furthermore, a political myth is always the myth of a particular group. It has as its hero or protagonist, not an individual, but a tribe, a nation, a race, a class or even a chance collection of exiles and immigrants. Individuals often figure in political myths, but they figure only as the representatives of their group or as the bearers of its destiny. In the last analysis, it is always the group which acts as the protagonist in a political myth.

Like all other myths, a political myth explains the circumstances of those to whom it is addressed. It renders their experience more coherent; it helps them understand the world in which they live. And it does so by enabling them to see their present condition as an episode in an on-going drama. A political myth may explain how the group came into existence and what its objectives are; it may explain what constitutes membership of the group and why the group finds itself in its present predicament; and, as often as not, it identifies the enemy of the group and promises eventual victory. It offers, in short, an account of the past and the future in the light of which the present can be understood. And as we would expect, this account is, not only an explanation, but also a practical argument.

A political myth may, for instance, establish the claim of a certain group to hegemony, sovereign independence or an extension of territory; it may help strengthen the solidarity of the group in the face of a major challenge; it may serve to encourage the resistance of an oppressed minority; or it may supply compelling arguments for the abolition of undesirable institutions. And, where the myth is the story of a political society already in existence, it may sanctify the constitution of that society, inspire its members with confidence in their destiny and glorify their achievements.

The view of political myth that I recommend does not amount to a theory. It is more in the nature of a definition. Perhaps this is just as well, for there are plenty of theories already in the field and most of them complicate matters more than is necessary. Myth-making is, after all, a fairly ordinary human activity. It is neither more nor less mysterious than fishing, war or scare-mongering. The difficulties we encounter in understanding myths are no different from those we encounter in understanding any other kind of human utterance. Myths are, quite simply, historical phenomena; and, if we wish to understand them, we had best attend to the concrete circumstances in which they occur.

Notes and References

Chapter One

1 Georges Sorel, *Reflections on Violence*, trans. T. E. Hulme and J. Roth, Collier Books, New York, 1961, pp. 41-2.
2 Ibid., p. 42.
3 Ibid., p. 78.
4 Ibid., p. 123.
5 Ibid., p. 50. See also R. Bastide, "Mythes et utopie", *Cahiers Internationaux de Sociologie*, VII, Jan.–June, 1960, no. 28, pp. 3–12.
6 Sorel, op. cit., p. 125.
7 Ibid., p. 46, footnote 31.
8 Ibid., p. 52.
9 H. D. Lasswell, *The Analysis of Political Behaviour, An Empirical Approach*, London, Routledge & Kegan Paul, (Fourth Impression) 1966, p. 197. See also H. D. Lasswell and A. Kaplan, *Power and Society, A Framework for Political Inquiry*, London, Routledge & Kegan Paul, 1952, pp. 116 ff.
10 C. J. Friedrich and Z. L. Brzezinski, *Totalitarian Dictatorship and Autocracy*, Frederick A. Praeger, New York, 1961, p. 99.
11 H. Diels & W. Kranz, *Die Fragmente der Vorsokratiker*, Weidmannsche Verlagsbuchhandlung, Zürich/Berlin, 1964, Xenophanes, B16.
12 See Sextus Empiricus, *Against the Physicists*, I, 14–25; Cicero, *De natura deorum*, II, 60; and Lucretius, *De rerum natura*, v. 1168 ff.
13 For examples, see Cicero, *De natura deorum*, II, 63–72.
14 For Eusebius's criticism, see his *Evangelicae Praeparatio*, Book iii. The preface to Bacon's *The Wisdom of the Ancients* (1609) contains a classic defence of the allegorical approach. See also Natale Conti, *Mythologiae sive explicationum fabularum* 1551. Also Bultmann's contribution in H. W. Bartsch, *Kerygma and Myth: a Theological Debate*, London, S.P.C.K., 1953.
15 H. J. Rose, *A Handbook of Greek Mythology*, University Paperbacks, Methuen, London, 1964, pp. 1–2.
16 F. Jacoby, *Die Fragmente der Griechischen Historiker*, Leiden & Berlin, 1923–58. Also, T. S. Brown, "Euhemerus and the Historians", *Harvard Theological Review*, 39:263, 1946.
17 See, for instance, Livy, *Ab urbe condita*, I, 6.
18 Dionysius of Halicarnassus, *The Roman Antiquities*, I, v.
19 Ibid., I, xxxix–xlv.
20 See Boileau's twelfth satire, *Sur l'equivoque*, written ca. 1705; Fontenelle's *De l'origine des fables*, 1724; and Giambattista Vico, *The New Science*, trans. & ed. by T. G. Bergin and M. H. Fisch, Cornell University Press, 1948, paragraphs 34 and 401 ff. For a good statement of Enlightenment Euhemerism, see Abbé Banier, *La Mythologie et les Fables exqliauées par l'Histoire*, Paris, 1739.
21 J. J. Bachofen, *Myth, Religion, and Mother Right: Selected Writings*, trans. R. Manheim, Routledge & Kegan Paul, London, 1967, p. 85. See also p. 185.

22 Ibid., pp. 116–19.
23 Ibid., pp. 94–100.
24 Ibid., p. 142.
25 Ibid., p. 91.
26 Ibid., pp. 129 and 149.
27 Ibid., p. 185.
28 Ibid., pp. 150–1.
29 Ibid., pp. 213–14.
30 Karl Marx & Friedrich Engels, *Selected Works in Two Volumes*, Foreign Languages Publishing House, Moscow, 1958, Vol. II, p. 175.
31 H. W. Bartsch, op. cit., pp. 10–11.
32 F. M. Müller, *Comparative Mythology, An Essay* . . . , Edited with Additional Notes and an Introductory Preface on Solar Mythology, by A. Smythe Palmer D.D., London, n.d., pp. 72–3.
33 Ibid., p. 82.
34 Ibid., pp. 82–100.
35 For an account of the controversy occasioned by Müller's work, see R. M. Dorson, "The Eclipse of Solar Mythology", in Thomas A. Sebeok (ed.), *Myth: A Symposium*, Indiana University Press, Midland Books, Bloomington, 1965.
36 G. W. Cox, *An Introduction to the Science of Comparative Mythology and Folklore*, London, 1881. For the satire on Müller, see Rev. R. F. Littledale, "The Oxford Solar Myth", published as an appendix to F. M. Müller, op. cit.
37 Edward Burnett Tylor, *The Origins of Culture*, Harper Torchbooks, New York, 1958, p. 392. (This is part one of Tylor's *Primitive Culture*, first published in 1871.)
38 Fontenelle, *De l'Origine des Fables*, edition critique par J.-R. Carré, Paris, 1932, pp. 15–16.
39 Andrew Lang, *Myth, Ritual and Religion*, London, 5th edition, 1929, p. 47.
40 Tylor, op. cit., p. 285
41 Lang, op. cit., p. 49.
42 Jane Ellen Harrison, *Themis: A Study of the Social Origins of Greek Religion*, London, Merlin Press, 1963, p. 328.
43 Ibid., pp. 42 ff.
44 Ibid., p. 329.
45 See S. H. Hooke (ed.), *Myth and Ritual*, Oxford, 1933; and A. M. Hocart, *The Life-giving Myth and Other Essays*, ed. with introduction by Lord Raglan, Methuen & Co., London, 1970.
46 Lord Raglan, "Myth and Ritual", in Thomas A. Sebeok, op. cit., p. 133.
47 T. H. Gaster, "Myth and Story", *Numen*, I, 1954, pp. 186 ff.
48 Clyde Kluckhohn, "Myths and Rituals: a General Theory", *Harvard Theological Review*, XXXV, 1942, pp. 45–79.
49 Ernst Cassirer, *The Myth of the State*, New Haven and London, Yale University Press, (fifth printing) 1963, pp. 284 ff. Friedrich & Brzezinski, op. cit., p. 171. Hannah Arendt, *The Origins of Totalitarianism*, London, George Allen & Unwin, 1967, pp. 377 ff.
50 Ernst Cassirer, *The Philosophy of Symbolic Forms, Vol. II, Mythical Thought*, trans. R. Manheim, Yale University Press, New Haven & London, 1966, pp. 31 and 73. For interpretations of myth similar to that of Cassirer, see H. and H.A. Frankfort, *Before Philosophy*, Penguin Books, 1961; John G. Gunnell, *Political Philosophy and Time*, Wesleyan University Press, Middletown, Connecticut, 1968; and Susanne K. Langer, *Philosophy in a New Key*, Harvard University Press, Cambridge, Mass., 1967.

51 Cassirer, op. cit., p. 35.
52 Frankfort, op. cit., p. 20.
53 Ibid., pp. 21–3; and Cassirer, op. cit., pp. 36–43.
54 Cassirer, op. cit., p. 64.
55 Frankfort, op. cit., p. 24; and Cassirer, op. cit., p. 45.
56 Frankfort, op. cit., p. 30; and Cassirer, op. cit., p. 98.
57 Cassirer, op. cit., pp. 110–11.
58 Ibid., pp. 74–5. See also Emile Durkheim, *The Elementary Forms of the Religious Life*, George Allen & Unwin, London, 1968, pp. 36–47.
59 Gunnell, op. cit., pp. 17–53.
60 Cassirer, *The Myth of the State*, op. cit., pp. 278–9.
61 Ibid., pp. 3–4.
62 Ibid., pp. 280–1.
63 Ibid., pl. 282.
64 Bachofen, op. cit., p. 75.
65 Müller, op. cit., p. 17.

Chapter Two

1 Robert C. Tucker, *Philosophy and Myth in Karl Marx*, Cambridge University Press, 1964, p. 219.
2 Norman Cohn, *The Pursuit of the Millennium*, Paladin, London, 1970, pp. 84–8.
3 Sigmund Freud, *Introductory Lectures on Psycho-Analysis*, Revised 2nd Edition, Hogarth Press, London, 1949, p. 82.
4 Ibid., pp. 95 ff. See also Sigmund Freud, *The Interpretation of Dreams*, trans. & ed. by James Strachey, George Allen & Unwin, London, 1967, chapters iii and iv.
5 Freud, *Introductory Lectures*, pp. 107–8.
6 Freud, *The Interpretation of Dreams*, chapter vi.
7 Freud, *Introductory Lectures*, p. 133–42. See also his *New Introductory Lectures on Psycho-Analysis*, trans. W. J. H. Sprott, The Hogarth Press, London, 1967, pp. 38–9.
8 Otto Rank, *The Myth of the Birth of the Hero*, Nervous and Mental Disease Monographs, New York, 1910; Karl Abraham, *Dreams and Myths: a Study in Race Psychology*, Nervous and Mental Disease Monographs, New York, 1913.
9 Karl Abraham, op. cit., pp. 36 ff.
10 Freud, *Introductory Lectures*, p. 196.
11 C. G. Jung & C. Kerenyi, *Introduction to a Science of Mythology*, Routledge & Kegan Paul, London, 1970, pp. 99 ff.
12 C. G. Jung, *Collected Works*, trans. R. F. C. Hull, 2nd Edition, Routledge & Kegan Paul, London, 1969, Vol. ix, Part I, pp. 3–4. See also Ibid., pp. 42 and 66.
13 Ibid., pp. 4–5 and 42–3.
14 Ibid., p. 66.
15 Ibid., p. 48; and Vol. vii, p. 69.
16 Jung, op. cit., Vol. ix, Part I, p. 6.
17 Ibid., p. 48. See also C. G. Jung & C. Kerenyi, op. cit., pp. 100–1, 105–6, and 114.
18 Jung, op. cit., Vol. ix, Part I, pp. 76 ff.
19 R. Chase, *Quest for Myth*, Baton Rouge, 1949, pp. 94–5. Also R. M. Dorson, "Theories of Myth and the Folklorist", in H. A. Murray (ed.), *Myth and Mythmaking*, New York, 1960, pp. 80–3.
20 Cassirer, *The Myth and the State*, op. cit., p. 47.

21 Lucien Lévy-Bruhl, *Les Fonctions Mentales dans les Sociétés Inférieures*, Paris, 1910, p. 1. See also Emile Durkheim, *The Elementary Forms of the Religious Life*, George Allen & Unwin, London, 1968, pp. 15–18.

22 For instance, he says of concepts that 'they correspond to the way in which this very special being, Society, considers the things of its own proper experience'. (Durkheim, op. cit., p. 435).

23 Bronislaw Malinowski, 'Myth in Primitive Psychology', in *Magic, Science and Religion and Other Essays*, Anchor Books, Doubleday & Co., New York, 1954, pp. 146 and 101. See also pp. 125–6 and 137.

24 Bronislaw Malinowski, *A Scientific Theory of Culture*, Galaxy Books, New York, 1960, pp. 39 and 83.

25 Clifford Geertz, 'Ideology as a Cultural System', in D. E. Apter (ed.), *Ideology and Discontent*, London, 1964, p. 56.

26 Ernest Nagel, *The Structure of Science*, Routledge & Kegan Paul, London, 1971, pp. 402 ff.

27 Malinowski, *A Scientific Theory of Culture*, pp. 36–42.

28 Quoted in Ernest Nagel, op. cit., p. 521.

29 Ernest Nagel, op. cit., pp. 408 ff. See also I. C. Jarvie, 'Limits of Functionalism and Alternatives to it in Anthropology', in D. Martindale (ed.), *Functionalism in the Social Sciences*, Monograph 5, The American Academy of Political and Social Science, Philadelphia, 1965.

30 E. R. Leach, *Political Systems of Highland Burma*, G. Bell & Sons, London, 1964 p. 278.

31 Claude Lévi-Strauss, *The Savage Mind*, Weidenfeld and Nicolson, London 1968, pp. 21–2.

32 Cassirer, op. cit., p. 282.

33 Ferdinand de Saussure, *Course in General Linguistics*, ed. by C. Bally & A. Sechehaye in collaboration with A. Riedlinger, trans. by W. Baskin, McGraw-Hill Book Co., New York, 1966, pp. 6–17 and 77.

34 Ibid., p. 81.

35 Ibid., pp. 67–8.

36 Ibid., p. 113.

37 Ibid., p. 120

38 Roman Jakobsen, 'Retrospect', in *Selected Writings*, Vol. 1. Mouton & Co., 'S-Gravenhage, 1962, p. 637. For an introduction to the work of the Prague School, see Josef Vachek, *The Linguistic School of Prague*, Indiana University Press, Bloomington & London, 1966.

39 Lévi-Strauss, *Structural Anthropology*, trans. Claire Jacobson and Brooke Grundfest Schoepf, Allen Lane the Penguin Press, London, 1968, p. 33.

40 Ibid., p. 59.

41 Ibid., p. 21.

42 Ibid., p. 65.

43 Ibid., p. 210.

44 Ibid., pp. 211 ff.

45 Lévi-Strauss, 'The Story of Asdiwal', in Edmund Leach (ed.), *The Structural Study of Myth and Totemism*, A.S.A. Monographs, Tavistock Publications, London, 1967.

46 Ibid., pp. 21 ff. See also *Structural Anthropology*, p. 229.

47 Lévi-Strauss, *Mythologiques: Le Cru et le Cuit*, Plon, Paris, 1964, p. 20.

48 Lévi-Strauss, *Structural Anthropology*, pp. 217 ff.

49 Ferdinand de Saussure, op. cit., p. 68.

50 As Roland Barthes, the literary critic, remarks: 'it is not for criticism to reconstitute the meaning of a work, but only its system, exactly as the linguist does not decipher the meaning of a sentence, but establishes the formal structure which allows the meaning to be conveyed'. Quoted

in Michael Lane (ed.), *Structuralism: A Reader*, Jonathan Cape, London, 1970, p. 37.

51 G. W. F. Hegel, *The Phenomenology of Mind*, trans. with introd. & notes by J. B. Baillie, 2nd edition, London, George Allen & Unwin Ltd., 1949, pp. 212–13.

52 H. W. Bartsch, *Kerygma and Myth: a Theological Debate*, London, S.P.C.K., 1953, p. 47; Ibid., p. 146; R. Guenon, *Apercus sur l'Initiation*, Paris, 1964, pp. 121–4.

53 Mircea Eliade, *Myth and Reality*, George Allen & Unwin, London, 1964, pp. 5–6.

54 Ibid., pp. 16–19 and 50–2.

55 Gaster, 'Myth and Story', *Numen*, I, 1954, p. 186.

56 M. I. Finley, 'Myth, Memory and History', *History and Theory*, IV, 1965, pp. 281–302. Finley argues that, in myths, we find expressed a practical attitude to the past. Myths contain a memory of men and events which are remembered only because they have some practical relevance in the present. However, by being so remembered, they cease to be historical men and events and acquire the timeless quality which, according to Finley, is the mark of a true myth.

Chapter Three

1 For the fragments of Fabius Pictor, see H. Peter, *Historicorum Romanorum Reliquiae*, 2 Vols., Teubner, Leipzig, 1914; and, for Naevius, E. H. Warmington (ed. & trans.), *Remains of Old Latin*, Vol. II, The Loeb Classical Library, London, 1967.

2 It was, at least, a native tradition; and, in historical times, it was associated with religious practices of great antiquity. On Romulus, see C. J. Classen, 'Zur Herkunft der Sage von Romulus and Remus', *Historia*, xii, 1963, pp. 447–57. It is possible that Romulus began his life as the eponymous ancestor of the patrician gens Romilia. See Einar Gjerstad, *Legends and Facts of Early Roman History*, Lund, 1962, pp. 39–40.

3 Felix Jacoby, *Die Fragmente der Griechischen Historiker*, E. J. Brill, Leiden, 1923–58, 560 F4 and 564 F5.

4 Cicero does not mention Remus in his account of Rome's origin, and neither do Sallust or Velleius Paterculus.

5 Felix Jacoby, op. cit., 4 F33–5.

6 Jean Berard, 'Nouvelles Notes sur la Légende de la Diaspora Troyenne', *Revue des Études Grecques*, lvii, 1944, pp. 71–86; Raymond Bloch, *The Origins of Rome*, London, 1964, p. 45; A. Alföldi, *Early Rome and the Latins*, Jerome Lectures, ser. 7, Ann Arbor, 1963, pp. 278 ff.; G. Karl Galinsky, *Aeneas, Sicily and Rome*, Princeton University Press, Princeton, 1969, pp. 122 ff.

7 Livy, v, 1–25. Galinsky, op. cit., p. 137.

8 Galinsky, op. cit., p. 139.

9 Ibid., p. 160.

10 Ibid., pp. 142–3 and 161.

11 Pausanius, I, xii, 2. Jacques Perret, *Les Origines de la Légende Troyenne de Rome* (281–31), Société d'Édition 'Les Belles Lettres', Paris, 1942, pp. 410 ff.

12 On Timaeus, see Perret, op. cit., pp. 345 ff. and 438 ff.

13 Ibid., pp. 419–27.

14 Ibid., pp. 452–4. Also Galinsky, op. cit., pp. 172–3.

15 Strabo, x, 462. Perret, op. cit., pp. 64–6.

16 Perret, op. cit., pp. 501 ff.
17 Nearly all commentators assume that Naevius included the episode in his account, but the evidence is slight and entirely circumstantial. There is no hint of the episode in any of the fragments surviving from Naevius's poem. None of the historians or poets prior to Virgil mention Aeneas's visit to Carthage. Indeed, many of them subscribe to an alternative tradition according to which Dido killed herself in order to avoid marriage with a local chieftain named Iarbas. None of the ancients, who had the full text of Naevius's poem, suggest that it was from him that Virgil borrowed the episode. Finally, the fact that the episode was generally regarded as a poetic fiction and never gained acceptance among historians suggests that it was known to be a relatively late innovation. See W. A. Camps, *An Introduction to Virgil's Aeneid*, Oxford University Press, London, 1969, pp. 78–80.
18 Pierre Grimal, *Hellenism and the Rise of Rome*, Weidenfeld and Nicolson, London, 1970, pp. 15 ff. See also Galinsky, op. cit., pp. 93–6, 161, and 171–8.
19 Suetonius, *Claudius*, 25, 3; Perret, op. cit., pp. 501–5 and Galinsky, op. cit., p. 187.
20 Livy, xxxvii, 37, 1–3.
21 Grimal, op. cit., pp. 16–17; Lidia Storoni Mazzolani, *The Idea of the City in Roman Thought*, trans. S. O'Donnell, Hollis & Carter, London, 1970, pp. 82–97.
22 Polybius, *Histories*, I, 1–4.
23 W. A. Camps, op. cit., pp. 18–19; Mazzolani, op. cit., p. 64.
24 See A. Alföldi, op. cit., passim.
25 Ennius, *Annales*, 486.
26 Hannah Arendt, *The Human Condition*, The University of Chicago Press, Chicago & London, 1958, Chapter 2.
27 Donald Earl, *The Moral and Political Tradition of Rome*, Thames & Hudson, London, 1967, p. 21.
28 For analyses of the political collapse of the Roman republic, see Ronald Syme, *The Roman Revolution*, Oxford University Press, Oxford, 1968; R. E. Smith, *The Failure of the Roman Republic*, Cambridge, 1955; and L. R. Taylor, *Party Politics in the Age of Caesar*, Berkeley, 1949.
29 R. E. Smith, op. cit., p. 37.
30 For a discussion of Caesar's monarchical ambitions, see J. Carcopino, *Les Étapes de l'Impérialisme Romain*, Paris, 1961; Mazzolani, op. cit., ch. vii; and E. Meyer, *Caesars Monarchie und das Principat des Pompeius*, Stuttgart, 1922.
31 Carcopino, op. cit., pp. 108 ff.
32 Cicero's account of the three kinds of constitution and their defects (*Rep.*, i, 44–70) seems largely based on Polybius, *Histories*, vi, 3–19.
33 The notion that, some time after the Second Punic War, Rome suffered a crisis which initiated a process of moral decline had become a commonplace by the time of Cicero. See Earl, op. cit., pp. 17–19.
34 Syme, op. cit., pp. 313–30; Mazzolani, op. cit., ch. viii.
35 On the use Augustus made of the Romulus legend, see J. Gagé, 'Romulus-Augustus', *Mélanges de l'École Française de Rome*, xlvii, 1930.
36 Mazzolani, op. cit., pp. 147–52. See Virgil, *Aeneid*, viii, 685 ff.
37 Earl, op. cit., p. 68.
38 Camps, op. cit., pp. 21–2.
39 Ibid., pp. 18–19
40 Throughout his works, Cicero is preoccupied with the coincidence of the state with the order of nature; and, in one place (*Rep.*, iii, 34), he notes that

there is a similarity 'between the overthrow, destruction, and extinction of a state, and the decay and dissolution of the whole universe'.

41 Lactantius, *Divine Institutes*, vii, 25
42 Rutilius Namatianus, *De reditu suo*, i, 49–140.

Chapter Four

1   D. R. Bultmann, *History and Eschatology*, The Gifford Lectures, Edinburgh, 1957, p. 23.
2   Eliade, *Myth and Reality*, op. cit., pp. 51–2.
3   Quoted in Bultmann, op. cit., p. 24.
4   Syme, op. cit., p. 218; see also J. Carcopino, *Virgile et le mystère de la ive. églogue*, Paris, 1930.
5   Mazzolani, op. cit., p. 153.
6   Lactantius, *Divine Institutes*, vii, 3. Lactantius's standpoint is not entirely consistent with the doctrine of divine omnipotence, but allowance must be made for the fact that he is here rebutting what he takes to be the pantheism of the Stoics.
7   Bultmann, op. cit., p. 36.
8   This is not to suggest that the abolition of politics is the main point of Christian eschatology. But politics is one of the essential features of the world destined to be abolished when the dawn of the Millennium breaks.
9   Norman Cohn, *The Pursuit of the Millennium*, London, 1957, pp. 14–15. Bultmann, op. cit., pp. 51–4.
10 François Hotman, *Francogallia*, 2nd edition, Cologne, 1574, *praefatio*.
11 Ibid., p. 33.
12 Ibid., p. 71.
13 J. W. Allen, *A History of Political Thought in the Sixteenth Century*, Methuen & Co., London, 1957, p. 309.
14 Christopher Hill, *Puritanism and Revolution*, Panther Books, London, 1968, pp. 64 ff.
15 Ibid., p. 73.
16 H. N. Brailsford, *The Levellers and the English Revolution*, ed. Christopher Hill, The Cresset Press, London, 1961, p. 130.
17 A. S. P. Woodhouse (ed.), *Puritanism and Liberty: Being the Army Debates (1647–9) from the Clarke Manuscripts with Supplementary Documents*, London, 1950, p. 96. See also Hill, op. cit., pp. 81 ff.
18 From *The Army's Petition* of 3 May, 1648, quoted in Brailsford, op. cit., p. 440.
19 George H. Sabine (ed.), *The Works of Gerrard Winstanley*, Cornell University Press, Ithaca, New York, 1941, pp. 304–5.
20 Comte de Boulainvilliers, *Essais sur la Noblesse de France Contenans une Dissertation sur son Origine & Abaissement*, Amsterdam, 1732, pp. 1–60. Also his *État de la France . . . Avec des Memoires sur l'Ancien Gouvernement de cette Monarchie jusqu'à Hugues Capet*, London, 1737, pp. 128 ff.
21 Boulainvilliers, *Essais sur la Noblesse . . .*, pp. 65–6.
22 Ibid., pp. 251 and 299–300.
23 Babeuf, *Textes Choisis*, Introduction et Notes par Claude Mazauric, Éditions Sociales, Paris, 1965, pp. 76–7; The Abbé Sieyès, *What is the Third Estate?*, trans. by M. Blondel, and edited with Historical Notes by S. E. Finer, Pall Mall Press, London & Dunmow, 1963, p. 60.
24 Jacques Barzun, *Race, a Study in Superstition*, Revised with a new Preface, New York, 1965, pp. 22–3; Hannah Arendt, *The Origins of Totalitarianism*, George Allen & Unwin, London, 1967, pp. 163–5.
25 Arendt, op. cit., p. 164.

26   Arthur de Gobineau, *The Inequality of the Human Races*, trans. by Adrian Collins, Howard Fertig, New York, 1967, p. 210.
27   Ibid., p. 25.
28   Quoted in Barzun, op. cit., p. 99.
29   Herbert Spencer, *The Man versus the State, With Four Essays on Politics and Society*, ed. with an introduction by Donald Macrae, Penguin Books, 1969, pp. 141 ff. P. Kropotkin, *Mutual Aid, a Factor of Evolution*, William Heinemann, London, 1904, passim.
30   We find no hint of it in, for instance, Gobineau or in any of his predecessors.
31   J. S. McCleland (ed.), *The French Right (From De Maistre to Maurras)*, Jonathan Cape, London, 1970, pp. 91–2.
32   Speech at Chemnitz, 2 April 1938 quoted in Alan Bullock, *Hitler, a Study in Tyranny*, Penguin Books, Harmondsworth, 1962, p. 398.
33   Adolph Hitler, *Mein Kampf*, trans. by Ralph Manheim, Houghton Miflin Co. Boston & The Riverside Press Cambridge, 1962, p. 285.
34   Ibid., p. 290.
35   Ibid., p. 303.
36   Ibid., p. 292.
37· Alfred Rosenberg, *Selected Writings*, Edited and introduced by Professor Robert Pois, Jonathan Cape, London, 1970, p. 97.
38   Houston Stewart Chamberlain, *The Foundations of the Nineteenth Century*, trans. by John Lees with an introduction by Lord Redesdale, 2 vols., London and New York, 1911, Vol. II, p. 23.
39   Rosenberg, op. cit., p. 96.
40   George L. Mosse (ed.), *Nazi Culture, Intellectual, Cultural and Social Life in the Third Reich*, translations by Salvator Attanasio and others, W. H. Allen, London, 1966, p. 326. See also Hitler, op. cit., pp. 509–10.
41   Rauschning, *Hitler Speaks*, quoted in Bullock, op. cit., p. 400.
42   Aristotle, *Politics*, 1278a20–21.
43   Karl Marx & Friedrich Engels, *Selected Works*, Vol. I, Foreign Languages Publishing House, Moscow, 1958, p. 40.
44   Karl Marx & Friedrich Engels, *The German Ideology*, Progress Publishers, Moscow, 1964, p. 44.
45   Karl Marx, *Capital*, Vol. I, Foreign Languages Publishing House, Moscow, 1961, chapters 14 and 15.
46   Karl Marx, *Early Writings*, trans. & ed. by T. B. Bottomore, C. A. Watts & Co., London, 1963, pp. 124–5.
47   Marx, *Capital*, Vol. I, p. 592. See also Ibid., pp. 10 and 270.
48   Marx, *Early Writings*, p. 71.
49   Arthur Bauer, quoted in Chalmers Johnson, *Revolutionary Change*, University of London Press, London, 1968, p. 1.
50   Friedrich Engels, *Anti-Dühring*, Foreign Languages Publishing House, Moscow, 1959, p. 391.
51   V. I. Lenin, *Collected Works*, Vol. 9, Foreign Languages Publishing House, Moscow, 1962, p. 113.
52   Marx & Engels, *The German Ideology*, p. 41.
53   Ibid., p. 44.
54   Ibid., p. 44.
55   Ibid., p. 60.
56   Ibid., p. 37.
57   Marx & Engels, *Selected Works*, Vol. I, p. 363.
58   Marx & Engels, *The German Ideology*, p. 62.
59   Marx, *Capital*, Vol. I, p. 751.
60   Marx & Engels, *Selected Works*, Vol. I, p. 34.

Chapter Five

1 As he says: 'Il s'agit de savoir quels mythes ont, aux diverses époques, poussé au renversement des situations existentes; les idéologies n'ont été que des traductions de ces mythes sous des formes abstraites.' *Matériaux d'une Théorie du Prolétariat*, Paris, 1919, p. 337.

2 Bartsch, op. cit., p. 11.

3 Ibid., p. 144.

4 H. J. Rose, *A Handbook of Greek Mythology, Including its Extension to Rome*, Methuen & Co., London, 1964, p. 11.

5 St Augustine, *Civitas Dei*, i. 20.

6 John of Salisbury, *The Statesman's Book*, trans. by John Dickinson, Russell & Russell, New York, 1963, pp. 7–8.

7 Tariq Ali (ed.), *New Revolutionaries, Left Opposition*, Peter Owen, London, 1969, p. 26.

8 Leo Strauss, *What is Political Philosophy? and Other Essays*, The Free Press, Gencoe, Ill., 1959, p. 10; Michael Oakeshott, *Experience and its Modes*, Cambridge University Press, Cambridge, 1966, p. 256.

9 Oliver Cromwell, *The Writings and Speeches*, ed. with an introduction and notes by W. C. Abbott, Harvard University Press, Cambridge, Mass, Vol. II, 1939, p. 483.

10 Ibid., Vol. I, 1937, p. 337.

11 Tariq Ali (ed.), op cit., pp. 18–19.

12 Michael Frayn, the *Observer*, London, 26 January, 1969.

13 Marx & Engels, *Selected Works*, op. cit., pp. 247–50.

14 Hobbes quoted in Christopher Hill, *Puritanism and Revolution*, Panther Books, London, 1968, p. 63.

15 Regis Debray, *Revolution in the Revolution?*, trans. by B. Ortiz, Penguin Books, Harmondsworth, 1968, p. 20.

16 Cohn, op. cit., p. 309.

17 Cicero, *In Catilinam*, I. 33. He significantly refers to Jupiter as 'you who were established by Romulus under the same auspices under which this city was established, rightly called by us the stayer of this city and empire...'

18 Johan Huizinga, *Homo Ludens*, Paladin, London, 1970, pp. 42 ff.

Bibliography

Bibliographical details relating to particular topics can be gleaned from the footnotes. The following is a short list of the books and articles the student is likely to find most useful in pursuing the subject of myth and political myth.

ABRAHAM, KARL, *Dreams and Myths: a Study in Race Psychology*, Nervous and Mental Disease Monograph, Series no. 15, New York, 1913.

ARENDT, HANNAH, *On Revolution*, Faber and Faber, London, 1963.

—— *The Origins of Totalitarianism*, George Allen & Unwin, London, 1967.

BACHOFEN, J. J., *Myth, Religion, and Mother Right, Selected Writings*, trans. Ralph Manheim, Routledge & Kegan Paul, London, 1967.

BANIER, THE ABBÉ, *La Mythologie et les Fables expliquées par l'Histoire*, Paris, 1738.

BARTHES, ROLAND, *Mythologies*, Selected and translated from the French by Annette Lavers, Jonathan Cape, London, 1972.

BARTSCH, H. W., *Kerygma and Myth: a Theological Debate*, S.P.C.K., London, 1953.

BASTIDE, R., 'Mythes et utopie', *Cahiers internationaux de Sociologie*, vii, Jan.–June, 1960, no. 28.

BROWN, TRUESDELL S., 'Euhemerus and the Historians', *Harvard Theological Review*, 39:263, 1946.

CASSIRER, ERNST, *Language and Myth*, trans. Susanne K. Langer, Dover Publications, New York, 1946.

—— *The Myth of the State*, Yale University Press, New Haven & London, 1963.

—— *The Philosophy of Symbolic Forms, Vol. II, Mythical Thought*, trans. Ralph Manheim, Yale University Press, New Haven & London, 1966.

COHN, NORMAN, *The Pursuit of the Millennium*, Paladin, London, 1970.

COX, GEORGE W., *An Introduction to the Science of Comparative Mythology and Folklore*, London, 1881.

DARDEL, ERIC, 'The Mythic', *Diogenes*, no. 7, 1954.

DORSON, RICHARD M. (ed.), *Peasant Customs and Savage Myths: Selections from the British Folklorists*, 2 vols., Routledge & Kegna Paul, London, 1968.

ELIADE, MIRCEA, *Myth and Reality*, George Allen & Unwin, London, 1964.

—— *Myths, Dreams and Mysteries, The Encounter between Contemporary Faiths and Archaic Reality*, trans. Philip Mairet, Fontana Library, London, 1968.

EVANS-PRITCHARD E. E., *Theories of Primitive Religion*, Oxford University Press, 1965.

FINLEY, M. I., 'Myth, Memory and History', *History and Theory*, iv, 1965.

FONTENELLE, *De l'Origine des Fables* (1724), Édition critique . . . par J.-R. Carré, Paris, 1932.

FRANKFORT, HENRI et al., *Before Philosophy*, Penguin Books, Harmondsworth, 1961.

FREUD, SIGMUND, *The Interpretation of Dreams*, trans. James Strachey, George Allen and Unwin, London, 1967.
—— *Totem and Taboo*, trans. James Strachey, Routledge & Kegan Paul, London, 1961.
FRIEDRICH, CARL J. and BRZEZINSKI, ZBIGNIEW K., *Totalitarian Dictatorship and Autocracy*, Frederick A. Praeger, New York & London, 1965.
GALINSKY, G. KARL, *Aeneas, Sicily, and Rome*, Princeton University Press, Princeton, New Jersey, 1969.
GASTER, T. H., 'Myth and Story', *Numen*, I, 1954.
GEORGES, ROBERT A. (ed.), *Studies on Mythology*, The Dorsey Press, Homewood, Ill., 1968.
GRANT, MICHAEL, *Myths of the Greeks and Romans*, Mentor Books, New York, 1964.
GUNNELL, JOHN G., *Political Philosophy and Time*, Wesleyan University Press, Middletown, Conn., 1968.
HARRISON, JANE ELLEN, *Themis: A Study of the Social Origins of Greek Religion*, Merlin Press, London, 1963.
HILL, CHRISTOPHER, *Puritanism and Revolution, Studies in Interpretation of the English Revolution of the 17th Century*, Panther Books, London, 1968.
HOBSBAWM, E. J., *Primitive Rebels: Studies in Archaic Forms of Social Movement in the 19th and 20th Centuries*, Manchester University Press, 1963.
HOCART, A. M., *The Life-Giving Myth and Other Essays*, edited with an introduction by Lord Raglan, Methuen & Co., London, 1970.
HOOKE, S. H. (ed.), *Myth and Ritual*, Oxford University Press, 1933.
JAMES, E. O., 'The Nature and Function of Myth', *Folklore*, 1957.
JUNG, C. G. and KERENYI, C., *Introduction to a Science of Mythology*, trans. by R. F. C. Hull, Routledge & Kegan Paul, London, 1970.
KIRK, G. S., *Myth, its Meaning and Functions in Ancient and Other Cultures*, Cambridge at the University Press, 1970.
KITAGAWA, JOSEPH M. and LONG, CHARLES H. (eds.), *Myths and Symbols, Studies in Honor of Mircea Eliade*, University of Chicago Press, Chicago and London, 1969.
KLUCKHOHN, CLYDE, 'Myths and Rituals: a General Theory', *Harvard Theological Review*, XXXV, 1942.
LANG, ANDREW, *Myth, Ritual and Religion*, 5th edition, London, 1929.
LASSWELL, HAROLD D. and KAPLAN, A., *Power and Society, A Framework for Political Inquiry*, Routledge & Kegan Paul, London, 1952.
LEACH, EDMUND, *Genesis as Myth and Other Essays*, Jonathan Cape, London, 1969.
—— *Political Systems of Highland Burma: a Study of Kachin Social Structure*, G. Bell and Sons, London, 1964.
—— (ed.), *The Structural Study of Myth and Totemism*, A.S.A. Monographs, Tavistock Publications, London, 1967.
LÉVI-STRAUSS, CLAUDE, *Mythologiques: Le Cru et le Cuit*, Plon. Paris, 1964.
—— *Structural Anthropology*, trans. Claire Jacobson and Brooke Grundfest Schoepf, Allen Lane the Penguin Press, London, 1968.
—— *The Savage Mind*, Weidenfeld and Nicolson, London, 1968.
—— 'A Confrontation', *New Left Review*, July–August, 1970, no. 62.
LÉVY-BRUHL, LUCIEN, *La Mythologie Primitive*, Presses Universitaires de France, Paris, 1963.
MALINOWSKI, BRONISLAW, *Magic, Science and Religion and Other Essays*, Doubleday Anchor Books, Garden City, New York, 1954.
—— *Sex, Culture and Myth*, Rupert Hart-Davie, London, 1963.
MELVILLE, J. and HERSKOWITZ, F. S., 'A Cross-Cultural Approach to Myth', *Dahomean Narrative*, Evanston, 1958.

MÜLLER, F. M., *Comparative Mythology*, ed. with additional notes and an introductory preface on solar mythology by A. Smythe Palmer D. D., London, n. d.

MURRAY, H. A. (ed.), *Myth and Mythmaking*, New York, 1960.

PERRET, JACQUES, *Les Origines de la Légende Troyenne de Rome*, (281–31), Sociéte d' Edition 'Les Belles Lettres', Paris, 1942.

PUHVEL, JAAN (ed.), *Myth and Law among the Indo-Europeans*, University of California Press, Berkeley, Los Angeles and London, 1970.

RANK, OTTO, *The Myth of the Birth of the Hero*, Nervous and Mental Disease Monographs, New York, 1910.

ROSE, H. J., *A Handbook of Greek Mythology, Including its Extension to Rome*, Methuen & Co., London, 1964.

SEBAG, LUCIEN, *Marxisme et Structuralisme*, Petite Bibliothèque Payot, Paris, 1964.

SEBEOK, THOMAS A., (ed.), *Myth: A Symposium*, Indiana University Press, Bloomington & London, 1965.

SOREL, GEORGES, *Reflections on Violence*, trans. T. E. Hulme and J. Roth, Collier Books, New York, 1961.

TYLOR, EDWARD BURNETT, *The Origins of Culture*, Harper Torchbooks, New York, Evenston, and London, 1958.

WORSLEY, PETER, *The Trumpet Shall Sound, A Study of 'Cargo' Cults in Melanesia*, Paladin, London, 1970.

Index

Abraham, Karl, 40–1: thesis regarding myths, 40–1
Actium, 86–7
Aeneas, 65–70, 78–9, 83, 86–8, 90, 122
Africanus, P. Cornelius Scipio, *see* Scipio, Publius Cornelius
Afrikaaner Myth of Great Trek, 16–17
Alba Longa, 72
Alcimus, 66
Alexander the Great, 69, 71, 78, 82
Allegorist, method of, 19
Allen, J. W., 100
Althusser, Louis, 52
American Independence Day, 30
American Myth of Founding Fathers, 16, 19, 91
American War of Independence, 16–17
Ammianus Marcellinus, 89
Amulius, 65
Ancus Marcius, 81
Anti-Semitism, 106
Appian, 84; Works, *The Civil Wars*, 84q.
Appropriation, process of, 44
Archetypes, 43–5
Arendt, Hannah, 104
Aristotle, 111
Aryan race, Myth of, 103–9, 138
Aryan tongue, 26
Augustine, St., 98, 127
Augustus, Caesar, 20, 65, 93, 126: version of Roman Foundation Myth, 86; Works, *Res Gestae*, 86q.

Babeuf, Francis Noel, 104
Bachofen, J. J., 22–5, 29, 36, 45; mother-right as dominating principle, 22; views on history, 22–3; matriarchal existence as mode of life, 22–3; Idealist theory, 24
Bacon, Francis, 18
Barthes, Roland, 52
Binary oppositions, 56

Boileau, Nicolas, 21
Bopp, Franz, 105
Boulainvilliers, Comte de, 103–4, 106
Brailsford, Henry, 101
'Bricolage', 52
Brutus, 81
Brzezinski, Zbigniewk, 16; views on myth, 16; implications of myth analysis, 16
Bultmann, D. R., 18, 25, 92, 122; real purpose of myth, 25

Caesar, Julius, 78, 82–3, 86, 93
Callias, 66
Camillus, 73
Carthage, 69–71, 84, 86, 89
Cassirer, Ernst, 14, 31–6, 130–1; status of myth as major symbolic form, 14; his theory of myths, 31–6; view that myths are collective representations, 46; features of mythical thought, 130; Works, *The Myth of the State*, 31q., 34q.; *The Philosophy of Symbolic Forms*, 31q., 33q.
Catholicism, 15
Cato, Marcus Aurelius, 62, 65, 77–8, 80–1; Works, *Origines*, 65q., 78q.
Chamberlain, Houston Stewart, 107–8; Works, *The Foundations of the Nineteenth Century*, 107q.
Christianity, 18, 93; fundamentally other-worldly, 94
Church Fathers, 126
Cicero, Marcus Tullius, 65, 71–3, 75–6, 86, 88–9, 135–7; his version of Roman Foundation Myth, 78–85; Works, *Republic*, 78q., 83q., *De natura deorum*, 72q.
City-state, life in, 74, 76, 89
Codes, 57–8, 122
Cohn, Norman, 14, 39, 98, 133–4; observations on psychic content of fantasies, 133–4; states myths grotesquely distort reality, 134